Adeline Knox

An American Girl Abroad

Adeline Knox

An American Girl Abroad

ISBN/EAN: 9783744692984

Printed in Europe, USA, Canada, Australia, Japan

Cover: Foto ©Andreas Hilbeck / pixelio.de

More available books at **www.hansebooks.com**

AN

AMERICAN GIRL ABROAD.

BY

ADELINE TRAFTON.

ILLUSTRATED

BY MISS L. B. HUMPHREY.

BOSTON:
LEE AND SHEPARD, PUBLISHERS.
NEW YORK:
LEE, SHEPARD AND DILLINGHAM.
1872.

Entered, according to the Act of Congress, in the year 1872,
By LEE AND SHEPARD,
In the Office of the Librarian of Congress, at Washington.

Electrotyped at the Boston Stereotype Foundry,
No. 19 Spring Lane.

I DEDICATE

𝔗𝔥𝔦𝔰 𝔑𝔢𝔠𝔬𝔯𝔡 𝔬𝔣 𝔓𝔩𝔢𝔞𝔰𝔞𝔫𝔱 𝔇𝔞𝔶𝔰

TO MY FATHER,

REV. MARK TRAFTON.

LIST OF ILLUSTRATIONS.

PAGE

I.

"At night we descended into the depths of the steamer to worship with the steerage passengers." FRONTISPIECE.

II.

"A dozen umbrellas were tipped up; the rain fell fast upon a dozen upturned, expectant faces." 57

III.

"At the word of command they struck the most extraordinary attitudes." 157

IV.

"Frowsy, sleepy, cross, and caring nothing whatever for the sun, moon, or stars, we stood like a company of Bedlamites, ankle deep in the wet grass upon the summit." . . . 176

V.

"Evidently the little old woman is going a journey." . . 196

VI.

"Together we stared at him with rigid and severe countenances." 240

CONTENTS.

CHAPTER I.

ABOARD THE STEAMER.

We two alone. — "Good by." — "Are you the captain of this ship?" — Wretchedness. — **The jolly Englishman and the Yankee.** — A sail! — The Cattle-man. — The Jersey-man whose bark was on the sea. — Church services under difficulties. — The sweet young English face. — Down into the depths to worship. — "Beware! I stand by the parson." — Singing to the fishes. — Green Erin. — One long cheer. — Farewell, Ireland. 13

CHAPTER II.

FIRST DAYS IN ENGLAND.

Up the harbor of Liverpool. — We all emerge as butterflies. — The Mersey tender. — Lot's wife. — "Any tobacco?" — "Names, please." — St. George's Hall. — The fashionable promenade. — The coffee-room. — The military man who showed the purple tide of war in his face. — The railway carriage. — The young man with hair all aflame. — English villages. — London. — No place for us. — The H. house. — The Babes in the Wood. — The party from the country. — We are taken in charge by the Good Man. — The Golden Cross. — Solitary confinement. — Mrs. B.'s at last. 27

CHAPTER III.

EXCURSIONS FROM LONDON.

Strange ways. — "The bears that went over to Charlestown." — The delights of a runaway without its dangers. — Flower show at the Crystal Palace. — Whit-Monday at Hampton Court. — A queen baby. — "But the carpets?" — Poor Nell Gwynne. — Vandyck faces. — Royal beds. — Lunch at the King's Arms. — O Music, how many murders have been committed in thy name! — Queen Victoria's home at Windsor. — A new "house that Jack built." — The Round Tower. — Stoke Pogis. — Frogmore. — The Knights of the Garter. — The queen's gallery. — The queen's plate. — The royal mews. — The wicker baby-wagons. — The state equipages. . . . 43

CHAPTER IV.

SIGHT-SEEING IN LONDON.

The Tower. — The tall Yankee of inquiring mind. — Our guide in gorgeous array. — War trophies. — Knights in armor. — A professional joke. — The crown jewels — The room where the little princes were smothered. — The "Traitor's Gate." — The Houses of Parliament. — What a throne is like. — The "woolsack." — The Peeping Gallery for ladies. — Westminster Hall and the law courts. — The three drowsy old women. — The Great Panjandrum himself. — Johnson and the pump. — St. Paul's. — Wellington's funeral car. — The Whispering Gallery. — The bell. 55

CHAPTER V.

AWAY TO PARIS.

The wedding party. — The canals. — New Haven. — Around the tea-table. — Separating the sheep from the goats. — "Will it

be a rough passage?"—Gymnastic feats of the little steamer.
—O, what were officers to us?—"Who ever invented earrings?"—Dieppe.—Fish-wives.—Train for Paris.—Fellow-passengers.—Rouen.—Babel.—Deliverance. . . . 68

CHAPTER VI.

THE PARIS OF 1869.

The devil.—Cathedrals and churches.—The Louvre.—Modern French art.—The Beauvais clock, with its droll, little puppets.—Virtue in a red gown.—The Luxembourg Palace.—The yawning statue of Marshal Ney.—Gay life by gaslight.—The Imperial Circus.—The Opera—How the emperor and empress rode through the streets after the riots.—The beautiful Spanish woman whose face was her fortune.—Napoleon's tomb. 76

CHAPTER VII.

SIGHTS IN THE BEAUTIFUL CITY.

The Gobelin tapestry.—How and where it is made.—Père La-Chaise.—Poor Rachel!—The baby establishment.—"Now I lay me."—The little mother.—The old woman who lived in a shoe.—The American chapel.—Beautiful women and children.—The last conference meeting.—"I'm a proofreader, I am." 90

CHAPTER VIII.

SHOW PLACES IN THE SUBURBS OF PARIS.

The river omnibuses.—Sèvres and its porcelain.—St. Cloud as it was.—The crooked little town.—Versailles.—Eugenie's "spare bedroom."—The queen who played she was a farmer's wife.—Seven miles of paintings.—The portraits of the presidents. 100

CHAPTER IX.

A VISIT TO BRUSSELS.

To Brussels. — The old and new city. — The paradise and purgatory of dogs. — The Hôtel de Ville and Grand Place. — St. Gudule. — The picture galleries. — Wiertz and his odd paintings. — Brussels lace and an hour with the lace-makers. — How the girls found Charlotte Brontë's school. — The scene of "Villette." 109

CHAPTER X.

WATERLOO AND THROUGH BELGIUM.

To Waterloo. — Beggars and guides. — The Mound. — Chateau Hougomont. — Victor Hugo's "sunken road." — Antwerp. — A visit to the cathedral. — A drive about the city. — An excursion to Ghent. — The funeral services in the cathedral. — "Poisoned? Ah, poor man!" — The watch-tower. — The Friday-market square. — The nunnery. — Longfellow's pilgrims to "the belfry of Bruges." 122

CHAPTER XI.

A TRIP THROUGH HOLLAND.

Up the Meuse to Rotterdam. — Dutch sights and ways. — The pretty milk-carriers. — The tea-gardens. — Preparations for the Sabbath. — An English chapel. — "The Lord's barn." — From Rotterdam to the Hague. — The queen's "House in the Wood." — Pictures in private drawing-rooms. — The bazaar. — An evening in a Dutch tea-garden. — Amsterdam to a stranger. — The "sights." — The Jews' quarter. — The family whose home was upon the canals. — Out of the city. — The pilgrims. 134

CHAPTER XII.

THE RHINE AND RHENISH PRUSSIA.

First glimpse of the Rhine. — Cologne and the Cathedral. — "Shosef in ter red coat." — St. Ursula and the eleven thousand virgins. — Up the Rhine to Bonn. — The German students. — Rolandseck. — A search for a resting-place. — Our Dutch friend and his Malays. — The story of Hildegund. — A quiet Sabbath. — Our Dutch friend's reply. — Coblentz. — The bridge of boats. — Ehrenbreitstein, over the river. — A scorching day upon the Rhine. — Romance under difficulties. — Mayence. — Frankfort. — Heidelberg. — The ruined castle. — Baden-Baden. — A glimpse at the gambling. — The new and the old " Schloss." — The Black Forest. — Strasbourg. — The mountains. 147

CHAPTER XIII.

DAYS IN SWITZERLAND.

The Lake of Lucerne. — Days of rest in the city. — An excursion up the Righi. — The crowd at the summit. — Dinner at midnight. — Rising before "the early worm." — The "sunrise" according to Murray. — Animated scarecrows. — Off for a tour through Switzerland. — The lake for the last time. — Grütlii. — William Tell's chapel. — Fluellen. — Altorf. — Swiss haymakers. — An hour at Amsteg. — The rocks close in. — The Devil's Bridge. — The dangerous road. — "A carriage has gone over the precipice!" — Andermatt. — Desolate rocks. — Exquisite wild flowers. — The summit of the Furka. — A descent to the Rhone glacier. — Into the ice. — Swiss villages. — Brieg. — The convent inn. — The bare little chapel on the hill. — To Martigny. 168

CHAPTER XIV.

AMONG THE EVERLASTING HILLS.

The quaint inn. — The Falls of the Sallenches, and the Gorge de Trient. — Shopping in a Swiss village. — A mule ride to Chamouni. — Peculiarities of the animals. — Entrance to the village. — Egyptian mummies lifted from the mules. — Rainy days. — Chamois. — The Mer de Glace. — "Look out of your window." — Mont Blanc. — Sallenches. — A diligence ride to Geneva. — Our little old woman. — The clownish peasant. — The fork in the road. — "Adieu." 189

CHAPTER XV.

LAST DAYS IN SWITZERLAND.

Geneva. — Calvin and jewelry. — Up Lake Leman. — Ouchy and Lausanne. — "Sweet Clarens."— Chillon. — Freyburg. — Sight-seers. — The Last Judgment. — Berne and its bears. — The town like a story. — The Lake of Thun. — Interlaken. — Over the Wengern Alp. — The Falls of Giessbach. — The Brunig Pass. — Lucerne again. 201

CHAPTER XVI.

BACK TO PARIS ALONE.

Coming home. — The breaking up of the party. — We start for Paris alone. — Basle, and a search for a hotel. — The twilight ride. — The shopkeeper whose wits had gone "a wool-gathering." — "Two tickets for Paris." — What can be the matter now? — Michel Angelo's Moses. — Paris at midnight. — The kind *commissionaire*. — The good French gentleman and his fussy little wife. — A search for Miss H.'s. — "Come up, come up." — "Can women travel through Europe alone?" A word about a woman's outfit. 220

AN
AMERICAN GIRL ABROAD.

CHAPTER I.

ABOARD THE STEAMER.

We two alone. — "Good by." — "Are you the captain of this ship?" — Wretchedness. — The jolly Englishman and the Yankee. — A sail! — The cattle-man. — The Jersey-man whose bark was on the sea. — Church services under difficulties. — The sweet young English face. — Down into the depths to worship. — "Beware! I stand by the Parson." — Singing to the fishes. — Green Erin. — One long cheer. — Farewell Ireland.

WE were going to Europe, Mrs. K. and I — alone, with the exception of the ship's company — unprotected, save by Him who watches over the least of his creatures. We packed our one trunk, upon which both name and nationality were conspicuously blazoned, with the necessaries, not luxuries, of a woman's toilet, and made our simple preparations for departure without a shadow of anxiety. "They who know nothing, fear nothing," said the paterfamilias, but added his consent and blessing. The rain poured in torrents as we drove down to the wharf. But floods could not have dampened our enthusiasm. A wild Irishman, with a suggestion of spirituous things in his air and general appearance, received us at the foot of the plank, one end of which touched earth, the other that unexplored region, the steamer. We followed the direction of his dirty finger, and there fell from our eyes, as it were, scales. In our ignorance, we had expected to find vast space, elegant surroundings, glass, glare, and glitter. We peered into the contracted quarters of the ladies' cabin. One side was filled with boxes and bundles; the other, with the prostrate form of an old lady, her head enveloped in a mammoth ruffle. We explored the saloon. The purser, with a wen and a gilt-banded cap on his head, was flying about like one distracted. An old gentleman similarly attired, with the exception of the wen,— the surgeon as we afterwards learned,— read a large book complacently in one corner, murmuring gently to himself. His upper teeth lacked fixity, so to speak; and as they fell with every word, he had the appearance of gnashing them continually at the invisible author. There was a hurrying to and fro of round, fresh-faced stewards in short jackets, a pushing and pulling of trunks and boxes, the sudden appearance and disappearance of nondescript individuals in slouched hats and water-proofs, the stirring about of heavy feet upon the deck above, the rattling of chains, the 'yo-ing' of hoarse voices, as the sailors pulled at the ropes, and, with it all, that sickening odor of oil, of dead dinners — of everything, so indescribable, so never-to-be-forgotten. Somewhat saddened, and considerably enlightened upon the subject of ocean steamers, we sought our state-room. It boasted two berths (the upper conveniently gained by mounting the stationary wash-stand), and a velvet-covered sofa beneath the large, square window, which last we learned, months later, when reduced to a port-hole for light and air, to appreciate. A rack and half a dozen hooks against the wall completed its furniture.

The time of departure arrived. We said the two little words that bring so many tears and heartaches, and ran up on the deck with the rain in our faces, and something that was not all rain in our eyes, for one last look at our friends; but they were hidden from sight. There comes to me a dim recollection of attempting to mount to an inaccessible place: of clinging to wet ropes with the intention of seeing the last of the land; of thinking it, after a time, a senseless proceeding, and of resigning ourselves finally to our berths and inevitable circumstances. Eight bells and the dinner bell; some one darkened our doorway.

"What's this? Don't give it up so. D'ye hear the dinner bell?"

"Are — are you the captain of this ship?" gasped Mrs. K., feebly, from the sofa.

"To be sure, madam. Don't give it up so."

Mrs. K. groaned. There came to me one last gleam of hope. What if it were possible to brave it out! In a moment my feet were on the floor, but whether my name were McGregor, or not, I could not tell. I made an abortive attempt after the pretty hood, prepared with such pleasant anticipations, and had a dim consciousness that somebody's hands tied it about my head. Then we started. We climbed heights, we descended depths indescribable, in that short walk to the saloon, and there was a queer feeling of having a windmill, instead of a head, upon my shoulders. A number of sympathizing faces were nodding in the most remarkable manner, as we reached the door, and the tables performed antic evolutions.

"Take me back!" and the berth and the little round stewardess received me. There followed a night of misery. One can form no idea, save from experience, of the horrors of the first night upon an ocean steamer. There are the whir, and buzz, and jar, and rattle, and bang of the screw and engine; the pitching and rolling of the ship, with the sensation of standing upright for a moment, and then of being made to rest comfortably upon the top of your head; the sense of undergoing internal somersaults, to say nothing of describing every known curve externally. You study physiology involuntarily, and doubt if your heart, your lungs, or indeed any of your internal organs, are firmly attached, after all; if you shall not lose them at the next lurch of the ship. Your head is burning with fever, your hands and feet like ice, and you feel dimly, but wretchedly, that this is but the beginning of sorrows; that there are a dozen more days to come. You are conscious of a vague wonder (as the night lengthens out interminably) what eternity *can* be, since time is so long. The bells strike the half hours, tormenting you with calculations which amount to nothing. Everything within the room, as well as without, swings, and rolls, and rattles. You are confident your bottles in the rack will go next, and don't much care if they do, though you lie and dread the crash. You are tormented with thirst, and the ice-water is in that same rack, just beyond your reach. The candle in its silver case, hinged against the wall, swings back and forth with dizzy motion, throwing moving distorted shadows over everything, and making the night like a sickly day. You long for darkness, and, when at last the light grows dim, until only a red spark remains and the smoke that adds its mite to your misery, long for its return. At regular intervals you hear the tramp, tramp, overhead, of the relieving watch; and, in the midst of fitful slumbers, the hoarse voices of the sailors, as the wind freshens and they hoist the sails, wake you from frightful dreams. At the first gray dawn of light come the swash of water and the trickling down of the stream against your window, with the sound of the holy-stones pushed back and forth upon the deck. And with the light — O, blessed light! — came to us a dawn of better things.

There followed days when we lay contented upon the narrow sofa, or within the contracted berths, but when to lift our heads was woe. A kind of negative blessedness — absence from misery. We felt as if we had lost our heart, our conscience, and almost our immortal soul, to quote Mark Twain. There remained to us only those principles and prejudices most firmly rooted and grounded. Even our personal vanity left us at last, and nothing could be more forsaken and appropriate than the plain green gown with its one row of military buttons, attired in which, day after day, I idly watched the faces that passed our door. "That's like you Americans," said our handsome young Irish doctor, pointing to these same buttons. "You can't leave your country without taking the spread-eagle with you!"

Our officers, with this one exception, were English. Our captain, a living representative of the traditional English sailor. Not young, save in heart; simple, unaffected, and frank in manner, but with a natural dignity that prevented undue familiarity, he sang about the ship from morning till night, with a voice that could carry no air correctly, but with an enjoyment delightful to witness — always a song suggested by existing circumstances, but with

"Cheer, boys, cheer; my mother's sold her mangle,"

when everything else failed. He was forward among the men on the deck with an eye to the wind, down below bringing fruit and comfort to the sick in the steerage, dealing out apples and oranges to the children, with an encouraging word and the first line of a song for everybody.

The life of the ship was an Englishman, with the fresh complexion almost invariably seen upon Englishmen, and forty years upon a head that looked twenty-five. He was going home after a short tour through the United States, with his mind as full of prejudices as his memorandum-book was of notes. He chanced, oddly enough, to room with the genuine Yankee of the company — a long, lean, good-natured individual from one of the eastern states, "close on ter Varmont," who had a way of rolling his eyes fearfully, especially when he glared at his food. He represented a mowing machine company, and we called him "the Mowing Machine Man." He accosted us one day, sidling up to our door, with, "How d'ye do to-day?"

"Better, thank you," I replied from the sofa.

"That's real nice. Tell ye what, we'll be glad to see the ladies out. How's yer mar?" nodding towards the berth from which twinkled Mrs. K.'s eyes. I laughed, and explained that our relations were of affection rather than consanguinity. His interest increased when he found we were travelling alone. He gave us his London address, evidently considering us in the light of Daniels about to enter the lions' den. "Ef ye have any trouble," said he, as he wrote down the street and number, "there's one Yankee'll stand up for ye." He amused the Englishman by calling out, "Hullo. D'ye feel *good* this morning?" "No," would be the reply, with a burst of laughter; "I feel awful wicked; think I'll go right out and kill somebody."

There was a shout one morning, "A sail! See the stars and stripes!" I had not raised my head for days, but staggered across the floor at that, and clinging to the frame, thrust my head out of the window. Yes, there was a ship close by, with the stars and stripes floating from the mast-head, I found, when the roll of the steamer carried my window to its level. "Seems good ter see the old rag!" I looked up to find the Mowing Machine Man gazing upon it with eyes all afloat. "I'd been a thinking," said he, "all them fellers have got somebody waiting for 'em over there," — our passengers were mostly English, — "but there wasn't nobody a waiting for me. Tell ye what," — and he shook out the folds of a red and yellow handkerchief, — " it does my heart good ter see the old flag." There was a bond of sympathy between us from that moment.

We had another and less agreeable specimen of

this free people — a tall, tough western cattle dealer, who quarrelled if he could find an antagonist, swore occasionally, drank liquor, and chewed tobacco perpetually, wore his trousers tucked into his long boots, his hands tucked into his pockets, and, to crown these attributes, believed in Andrew Johnson! — a middle-aged man, with soft, curling brown hair above a face that could be cruelly cold and hard. His hair should have been wire; his blue eyes were steel. But hard as was his face, it softened and smoothed itself a little at sight of the sick women. He paused beside us one day with a rough attempt to interest and amuse by displaying a knife case containing a dozen different articles. "This is ter take a stun out of a hoss's huf, and this, d'ye see, is a tooth-pick;" putting it to immediate use by way of explanation. At the table he talked long and loud upon the rinderpest, and other kindred and appetizing topics. "I've been a butcher myself," he would say. "I've cut up hundreds o' critters. What part of an ox, now, d'ye think that was taken from?" pointing to the joint before him, and addressing a refined, delicate-faced old gentleman across the table, who only stared in silent horror.

But even the "Cattle Man" was less marked in his peculiarities than the "Jersey Man," a melancholy-eyed, curly-wigged individual from the Jersey shore, who wore his slouched hat upon one side of his head, and looked as though he were doing the rakish lover in some fifth-rate theatre; who was "in the musical line myself; Smith and Jones's organs, you know; that's me;" and who, being neither Smith nor Jones, we naturally concluded must be the organ. He recited poetry in a loud tone at daybreak, and discussed politics for hours together, arguing in the most satisfactory manner with the principles, and standing most willingly upon the platform, of everybody. He assumed a patronizing air towards the Mowing Machine Man. "Well, you *are* a green Yankee," he would say; "lucky for you that you fell in with me;" to which the latter only chuckled, "That's so." He had much to tell of himself, of his grandmother, and of his friends generally, who came to see him off; "felt awfully, too," which we could hardly credit; rolled out snatches of sentimental songs, iterating and reiterating that his bark was on the sea,—and a most disagreeable one we found it; wished we had a piano on board, to which we murmured, "The Lord forbid;" and hoped we should soon be well enough to join him in the "White Squall." He was constantly reminding us that we were a very happy family party, so "congenial," and evidently agreed with the Mowing Machine Man, who said, "They're the best set of fellows I ever see. They'll tell ye anything."

We numbered a clergyman among us, of course. "Always a head wind when there's a parson aboard," say the sailors. So this poor dyspeptic little man bore the blame of our constant adverse winds. Nothing more bigoted, more fanatical than his religious belief could be imagined. You read the terrors of the Lord in his eye; and yet he won respect, and something more, by his consistency and zeal. Earnestness will tell. "The parson will have great influence over the Cattle Man," the captain said, Sabbath morning, as we were walking the deck. "The Cattle Man?"

"Yes, the parson will get a good hold of him." Just then, as if to prove the old proverb true, that his satanic majesty is always in the immediate neighborhood when his character is under discussion, the Cattle Man and Jersey came up the companion-way. "If you please, captain," said the former, "we are a committee to ask if the parson may preach to the steerage people to-night." "Certainly," was the reply; "I will attend myself." They thanked him, and went below, leaving me utterly amazed. They were the last men upon the ship whom one would have selected as a committee upon spiritual things!

The church service for the cabin passengers was held in the saloon. A velvet cushion upon one end of the long table constituted the pulpit, before which the minister stood, holding fast to the rack on either side, and bracing himself against the captain's chair in the rear. Even then he made, involuntarily, more bows than any ritualist, and the scripture, "What went ye out for to see? A reed shaken by the wind?" would present itself. The sailors in their neat dress filed in and ranged themselves in one corner. The stewards gathered about the door, one, with face like an owl, most conspicuous. The passengers filled their usual seats, and a delegation from the steerage crept shyly into the unoccupied space — women with shawls over their heads and babies in their arms, shock-headed men and toddling children, but all with an evident attempt at appropriate dress and manner. Among them was one sweet young English face beneath an old crape bonnet. A pair of shapely hands, which the shabby black gloves could not disguise, held fast a little child. Widowhood and want in the old world; what was waiting her in the new? The captain read the service, and all the people responded. The women's eyes grew wet at the sound of the familiar words. The little English widow bent her face over the head of the child in her lap, and something glistened in its hair. Our sympathies grew wide, and we joined in the prayer for the queen, that she might have victory over her enemies, and even murmured a response to the petition for Albert Edward and the nobility, dimly conscious that they needed prayers. The good captain added a petition for the president of the United States, to which the Mowing Machine Man and I said, "Amen." Then the minister, having poised himself carefully, read a discourse, sulphurous but sincere; the Mowing Machine Man thrusting his elbow into my side in a most startling manner at every particularly blue point. We were evidently in sympathy; but I could have dispensed with the expression of it. We closed with the doxology, standing upon our feet and swaying back and forth as though it had been a Shaker chant, led by an improvised choir and the Jersey Man.

At night we descended into the depths of the steamer to worship with the steerage passengers. It was like one of Rembrandt's pictures — the darkness, the wild, strangely-attired people, the weird light from the lanterns piercing the gloom, and bringing out group after group with fearful distinctness; the pale, earnest face of the preacher, made almost unearthly by the glare of the yellow light — a face with its thin-drawn lips, its eyes like coals of fire such as the flames of martyrdom lit once, I imagine. Close beside him stood the Cattle Man, towering like Saul above the people, and with an air that plainly said, "Beware—I stand by the parson."

"There is a land of pure delight,"

repeated the minister; and in a moment the words rolled out of the Cattle Man's mouth while he beckoned with his long arm for the people to rise. Throwing back his head, he sang with an unction indescribable, verse after verse, caught doubtless at some western camp-meeting, where he had tormented the saints. One after another took up the strain. Clear and strong came the tones from every dark corner, until, like one mighty voice, while the steamer rolled and the waves dashed against its sides, rose the words

"Not Jordan's stream, nor death's cold flood,
Shall fright us from that shore."

A great stillness fell upon the people as the minister gave out his text, and began his discourse. He had lacked freedom in the saloon, but here he forgot everything save the words given him; hard words they seemed to me, containing little of the love of God. I glanced at the Mowing Machine Man, who had made a seat of half a barrel under the stairs. He winked in a fearful manner, as though he would say, "Just see how he's a goin' on!" But the people received it gladly. One after another of the sailors crept down the stairs and stood in the shadow. I watched them curiously. It may be that this stern, hard doctrine suited these stern, hard men. It made me shudder.

But the record of all these days would have no end. How can I tell of the long, happy hours, when more than strength, when perfect exhilaration, came to us; when existence alone was a delight? To sit upon the low wheel-house, with wraps and ribbons and hair flying in the wind, while we sang,—

"O, a life on the ocean wave!"

to admiring fishes; to watch the long, lazy swell of the sea, or the spray breaking from the tops of the white caps into tiny rainbows; to walk the rolling deck for hours with never a shadow of weariness; to cling to the flag-staff when the stern of the ship rose in the air then dropped like a heavy stone into the sea, sending the spray far over and above us; to count the stars at night, watching the other gleaming phosphorescent stars that seemed to have fallen from heaven upon the long wake of the steamer,— all this was a delight unspeakable.

One morning, when the land seemed a forgotten dream, we awoke to find green Erin close beside us. All the day before the sea-gulls had been hovering over us — beautiful creatures, gray above and white beneath, clouds with a silver lining. Tiny land birds, too, flew about us, resting wearily upon the rigging. The sea all at once became like glass. It seemed like the book of Revelation when the sun shone on it,— the sea of glass mingled with fire. For a time the land was but a line of rock, with martello towers perched upon the points. On the right, Fastnet Rock rose out of the sea, crowned with a light-house; then the gray barren shore of Cape Clear Island, and soon the sharp-pointed Stag Rocks. It is a treacherous coast. "I've been here many a night," said the captain, as he gave us his glass, "when I never expected to see morning." And all the while he was speaking, the sea smiled and smiled, as though it could never be cruel.

We drew nearer and nearer, until we could see the green fields bounded by stone walls, the white, winding roads, and little villages nestling among the hills. Towards noon the lovely harbor of Queenstown opened before us, surrounded and almost shut in by rocky islands. Through the glass we could see the city, with its feet in the bay. We were no longer alone. The horizon was dotted with sails. Sometimes a steamer crossed our wake, or a ship bore down upon us. We hoisted our signals. We dipped our flag. The sailors were busy painting the boats, and polishing the brass till it shone again. Now the tender steams out from Queenstown. The steerage passengers in unwonted finery, tall hats and unearthly bonnets, and one in a black silk gown, are running about forward, shaking hands, gathering up boxes and bundles, and pressing towards the side which the tender has reached. There are the shouting of orders, the throwing of a rope, and in a moment they are crowding the plank. One long cheer, echoed from the stern of our steamer, and they are off.

All day we walked the deck; even the sick crawled up at last to see the panorama. We still lingered when night fell, and we had turned away from the land to strike across the channel, and the picture rests with me now; the purple sky with one long stretch of purple, hazy cloud, behind which the sun went down; the long, low line of purple rock, our last glimpse of Ireland, and the shining, purple sea, with not a ripple upon its surface.

CHAPTER II.

FIRST DAYS IN ENGLAND.

Up the harbor of Liverpool. — We all emerge as butterflies. — The Mersey tender. — Lot's wife. — "Any tobacco?" — "Names, please." — St. George's Hall. — The fashionable promenade. — The coffee-room. — The military man who showed the purple tide of war in his face. — The railway carriage. — The young man with hair all aflame — English villages. — London. — No place for us. — The H. house. — The Babes in the Wood. — The party from the country. — We are taken in charge by the Good Man. — The Golden Cross. — Solitary confinement. — Mrs. B.'s at last.

WE steamed up the harbor of Liverpool the next morning. New Brighton, with its green terraces, its Chinese-pagoda villas, spread out upon one side, upon the other that solid wall of docks, the barricade that breaks the constant charges of the sea, with the masts of ships from every land for an abattis. The wraps and shapeless garments worn so long were laid aside; the pretty hood which had, like charity, covered so many sins of omission, hidden, itself, at last, the soft wool stiffened with the sea spray, the bright colors dimmed by smoke, and soot, and burning sun. We crept shyly upon the deck in our unaccustomed finery, as though called at a moment's notice to play another woman's part, half-learned. Not in us alone was the transformation. The girl in blue had blossomed into a a bell — a blue bell. The Cattle Man, his hands released at last from the thraldom of his pockets, stalked about, funereal, in wrinkled black. A solferino neck-tie and tall hat of a pre-Adamite formation transmogrified our Mowing Machine friend. Nondescripts, that had lain about the deck wrapped in cocoons of rugs and shawls, emerged suddenly — butterflies! A painful courtesy seized us all. We had doffed the old familiar intercourse with our sea-garments. We gathered in knots, or stood apart singly, mindful at last of our dignity.

The Mersey tender (a tender mercy to some) puffed out to meet us, and we descended the plank as those who turn away from home, leaving much of our thoughts, and something of our hearts, within the ship. It had been such a place of rest, of blessed idleness! Only when our feet touched the wharf did we take up the burden of life again. There were the meeting of friends, in which we had no part; the maelstrom of horses, and carts, and struggling humanity, in which we found a most unwilling place; and then we followed fast in the footsteps of the Mowing Machine Man, who in his turn followed a hair-covered trunk upon the shoulders of a stout porter, our destination the custom-house shed close by. For a moment, as we were tossed hither and thither by the swaying mass, our desires followed our thoughts to a certain sheltered nook, upon a still, white deck, with the sunbeams slanting down through the furled sails above, with the lazy, lapping sea below, and only our own idle thoughts for company. Then we remembered Lot's wife.

There was a little meek-faced custom-house officer in waiting, with a voice so out of proportion to his size, that he seemed to have hired it for the occasion, or come into it with his uniform by virtue of his office. "Any tobacco?" he asked, severely, as we lifted the lid of our one trunk. We gave a virtuous and indignant negative. That was all. We might go our several ways now unmolested. One fervent expression of good wishes among our little company, while we make for a moment a network of clasped hands, and then we pass out of the great gates into our new world, and into the clutches of the waiting cabmen. By what stroke of good fortune we and our belongings were consigned to one and the same cab, in the confusion and terror of the moment, we did not know at the time. It was clearly through the intervention of a kind fellow-passenger, who, seeing that amazement enveloped us like a garment, kindly took us in charge. The dazed, as well as the lame and lazy, are cared for, it seems. By what stroke of good fortune we ever reached our destination, we knew still less. Our cab was a triumph of impossibilities, uncertainties, and discomfort. Our attenuated beast, like an animated hoop skirt, whose bones were only prevented, by the encasing skin, from flying off as we turned the corners, experienced hardly less difficulty in drawing his breath than in drawing his load. We descended at the entrance to the hotel as those who have escaped from imminent peril. We mounted the steps — two lone, but by no means lorn, damsels, two anxious, but by no means aimless females, knowing little of the world, less of travelling, and nothing whatever of foreign ways. Our very air, as we entered the door, was an apology for the intrusion.

"Names, please," said the smiling man in waiting, opening what appeared to be the book of fate. We added ours to the long list of pilgrims and strangers who had sojourned here, dotting our i's and crossing our t's in the most elegant manner imaginable. If any one has a doubt as to our early advantages, let him examine the record of the Washington Hotel, Liverpool. The heading, "Remarks," upon the page, puzzled us. Were they to be of a sacred or profane nature? Of an autobiographical character? Were they to refer to the dear land we had just left? Through some political throes she had just brought forth a ruler. Should we add to the U. S. against our names, "As well as could be expected"? We hesitated, — and wrote nothing. Up the wide stairs, past the transparency of Washington — in the bluest of blue coats, the yellowest of top boots, and an air of making the best of an unsought and rather ridiculous position — we followed the doily upon the head of the pretty chambermaid to our wide, comfortable room, with its formidable, high-curtained beds. The satchels and parcels innumerable were propped carefully into rectitude upon the dressing table, under the impression that the ship would give a lurch; and then, gazing out through the great plate glass windows upon the busy square below, we endeavored to compose our perturbed minds and gather our scattered wits.

It is not beautiful, this great city of Liverpool, creeping up from the sea. It has little to interest a stranger aside from its magnificent docks and warehouses.

There are mammoth truck horses from Suffolk, with feet like cart wheels; there is St. George's Hall, the pride of the people, standing in the busy square of the same name, with a statue of the saint himself — a terror to all dragons — just before it. It is gray, many columned, wide stepped, vast in its proportions. Do you care for its measurement? Having seen that, you are ready to depart; and, indeed, there is nothing to detain one here beyond a day of rest, a moment to regain composure after the tossing of the sea. There are some substantial dwellings, — for commerce has its kings, — and some fine shops, — for commerce also has its queens, — and one fine drive, of which we learned too late. The air of endurance, which pervades the whole city, as it does all cities in the old world, impresses one greatly, as though they were built for eternity, not time; the founders having forgotten that here we are to have no continuing city. In the new world, man tears down and builds up. Every generation moulds and fashions its towns and cities after its own desires, or to suit its own means. Man is master. In the old world, one generation after another surges in and out of these grim, gray walls, leaving not so much as the mark the waves leave upon the rocks. Unchanged, unchanging, they stand age after age, time only softening the hard outlines, deepening the shadows it has cast upon them, and so bringing them into a likeness of each other that they seem to have been the design of one mind, the work of one pair of hands, and hardly of mortal mind or hands at that. They seem to say to man, "We have stood here ages before you were born. We shall stand here ages after you are forgotten."

They must be filled with echoes, with ghosts, and haunting memories.

Bold Street, a tolerably narrow and winding way, in which many are found to walk, — contrary to all precedent, — boasts the finest shops. Here the Lancashire witches, as the beauties of the county are called, walk, and talk, and buy gewgaws of an afternoon. It was something strange to us to see long silken skirts entirely destitute of crinoline, ruffle, or flounce, trailed here through mud and mire, or raised displaying low Congress gaiters, destitute of heels. For ourselves, if we had been the king of the Cannibal Islands, we could hardly have attracted more attention than we did in our plain, short travelling suits and high-heeled boots. It grew embarrassing, especially when our expression of unqualified benevolence drew after us a train of beggars. They crossed the street to meet us. They emerged from every side street and alley, thrusting dirty hands into our faces, and repeating twice-told tales in our ears, until we were thankful when oblivion and the shadow of the hotel fell upon us.

We dined in the coffee-room, — that comfortable and often delightfully cosy apartment fitted with little tables, and with its corner devoted to books, to papers and conversation, — that combination of dining, tea and reading-room unknown to an American hotel, — sacred to the sterner sex from all time, and only opened to us within a few years, — the gates being forced then, I imagine, by American women, who will not consent to hide their light under a bushel, or keep to some far-away corner, unseeing and unseen. English women, as a rule, take their meals in their own private parlors. Perhaps because English men generally desire the flowers intrusted to their fostering care to blush unseen. It may be better for the gardeners; it may be better for the flowers — I cannot tell; but we dined in the coffee-room, as Americans usually do. One of the *clergymen*, who attend at such places, received our order. It was not so very formidable an affair, after all, this going down by ourselves; or would not have been, if the big-eyed waiter, who watched our every movement, would have left us, and the military man at the next table, who showed "the purple tide of war," or something else, in his face, and blew his nose like a trombone, ceased to stare. As it was, we aired our most elegant table manners. We turned in our elbows and turned out our toes, — so to speak, — and ate our mutton with a grace that destroyed all appetite. We tried to appear as though we had frequently dined in the presence of a whole battalion of soldiery, under the scrutiny of innumerable waiters, — and failed, I am sure. "With verdure clad" was written upon every line of our faces. The occasion of this cross fire we do not know to this day. Was it unbounded admiration? Was it spoons?

Having brushed off the spray of the sea, having balanced ourselves upon the solid earth, having seen St. George's Hall, there was nothing to detain us longer, and the next morning we were on our way to London. We had scrutinized our bill, — which might have been reckoned in pounds, ounces, and pennyweights, for aught we knew to the contrary, — and informed the big-eyed waiter that it was correct. We had also offered him imploringly our largest piece of silver, which he condescended to accept; and having been presented with a ticket and a handful of silver and copper by the porter who accompanied us to the station across the way, in return for two or three gold pieces, we shook off the dust of Liverpool from our feet, turned our eyes from the splendors of St. George's Hall, and set our faces steadfastly towards our destination. There was a kind of luxury, notwithstanding our prejudices, in this English railway carriage, with its cushions all about us, even beneath our elbows; a restfulness unknown in past experience of travel, in the ability to turn our eyes away from the flying landscape without, to the peaceful quiet, never intruded upon, within. We did not miss the woman who will insist upon closing the window behind you, or opening it, as the case may be. Not one regret had we for the "B-o-s-t-o-n papers!" nor for the last periodical or novel. The latest fashion gazette was not thrown into our lap only to be snatched away, as we became interested in a plan for rejuvenating our wardrobe; nor were we assailed by venders of pop corn, apples, or gift packages of candy. Even the blind man, with his offering of execrable poetry, was unknown, and the conductor examined our tickets from outside the window. Settling back among our cushions, while we mentally enumerated these blessings of omission, there came a thought of the perils incurred by solitary females locked into these same comfortable carriages with madmen. If the danger had been so great for one solitary female, what must it be for two, we thought with horror. We gave a quick glance at our

FIRST DAYS IN ENGLAND.

fellow-passenger, a young man with hair all aflame. Certainly his eyes did roll at that moment, but it was only in search of a newsboy; and when he exclaimed, like any American gentleman, "Hang the boy!" we became perfectly reassured. He proved a most agreeable travelling companion. We exchanged questions and opinions upon every subject of mutual interest, from the geological formation of the earth to the Alabama claims. I can hardly tell which astonished us most, his profound erudition or our own. Now, I have not the least idea as to whether Lord John Russell sailed the Alabama, or the Alabama sailed of itself, spontaneously; but, whichever way it was, I am convinced it was a most iniquitous proceeding, and so thought it safe to take high moral ground, and assure him that as a nation we could not allow it to go unpunished. You have no idea what an assistance it is, when one is somewhat ignorant and a good deal at a loss for arguments, to take high moral ground.

When we were weary of discussion, when knowledge palled upon our taste, we pulled aside the little blue curtain, and gave ourselves up to gazing upon the picture from the window. I doubt if any part of England is looked upon with more curious eyes than that lying between Liverpool and London. It is to so many Americans the first glimpse of strange lands. Spread out in almost imperceptible furrows were the velvet turfed meadows, the unclipped hedges a mass of tangled greenness between. For miles and miles they stretched away, with seldom a road, never a solitary house. The banks on either side were tufted with broom and yellow with gorse; the hill-sides in the distance, white with chalk, or black with the heather that would blossom into purple beauty with the summer. We rushed beneath arches festooned, as for a gala-day, with hanging vines. Tiny gardens bloomed beside the track at every station, and all along the walls, the arched bridges, and every bit of stone upon the wayside, was a mass of clinging, glistening ivy. Not the half-dead, straggling thing we tend and shield so carefully at home, with here and there a leaf put forth for very shame. These, bright, clear-cut, deep-tinted, crowded and overlapped each other, and ran riot over the land, transforming the dingy, mildewy cottages, bits of imperishable ugliness, into things of beauty, if not eternal joys. Not in the least picturesque or pleasing to the eye were these English villages; straggling rows of dull red brick houses set amidst the fields — dirty city children upon a picnic — with a foot square garden before each door, cared for possibly, possibly neglected. A row of flower-pots upon the stone ledge of every little window, a row of chimney-pots upon the slate roof of every dwelling. Sometimes a narrow road twisted and writhed itself from one to another, edged by high brick walls, hidden beneath a weight of ivy; sometimes romantic lanes, shaded by old elms, and green beyond all telling. The towns were much the same, — outgrown villages. And the glimpse we caught, as we flew by, so far above the roofs often that we could almost peep down upon the hearths through the chimney tops, was by no means inviting.

Dusk fell upon us with the smoke, and mist, and drizzling rain of London, bringing no anxiety; for was there not, through the thoughtfulness of friends, a place prepared for us? Our pleasant acquaintance of the golden locks forsook his own boxes, and bundles, and innumerable belongings to look for our baggage, and saw us safely consigned to one of the dingy cabs in waiting. I trust the people of our own country repay to wanderers there something of the kindness which American women, travelling alone, receive at the hands of strangers abroad. It was neither the first nor the last courtesy proffered most respectfully, and received in the spirit in which it was offered. There is a deal of nonsense in the touch-me-not air with which many go out to see the world, as there is a deal of folly in the opposite extreme. But these acquaintances of a day, the opportunity of coming face to face with the people in whose country you chance to be, of hearing and answering their strange questions in regard to our government, our manners and customs, as well as in displaying our own ignorance in regard to their institutions, in giving information and assistance when it is in our power, and in gratefully receiving the same from others, — all this constitutes one of the greatest pleasures of journeying.

Our peace of mind received a rude shock, when, after rattling over the pavings around the little park in Queen's Square, and pulling the bell at Mr. B.'s boarding-house, we found that we were indeed expected, but indefinitely, and no place awaited us. We had forgotten to telegraph. It was May, the London season, and the hotels full. "X. told us you were coming," said the most lady-like landlady, leading us into the drawing-room from the dank darkness of the street. There was a glow of red-hot coals in the grate, a suggestion of warmth and comfort in the bright colors and cosy appointments of the room — but no place for us. "I'm very sorry; if you had telegraphed — but we can take you by Monday certainly," she said. I counted my fingers. Two days. Ah! but we might perish in the streets before that. Everything began to grow dark and doleful in contemplation. Some one entered the room. The landlady turned to him: "O, here is the good man to whose care you were consigned by X." We gave a sigh of relief, as we greeted the Good Man, for all our courage, like the immortal Bob Acres's, had been oozing from our finger ends. And if we possess one gift above another, it is an ability to be taken care of. "Do you know X.?" asked another gentleman, glancing up from his writing at the long, red-covered table. "We travelled with him," nodding towards his daughter, whose feet touched the fender, "through Italy, last winter." "Indeed —"

"I'll just send out to a hotel near by," interrupted kind Mrs. B., "and see if you can be accommodated a day or two." How very bright the room became! The world was not hollow, after all, nor our dolls stuffed with sawdust. Even the cabman's rattle at the knocker, and demand of an extra sixpence for waiting, could not disturb our serenity. The messenger returned. Yes; we could be taken in (?) at the H. house; and accepting Mrs. B.'s invitation to return and spend the evening, we mounted to our places in the little cab, as though it had been a triumphal car, and were whizzed around the corner at an alarming pace by the impatient cabman.

I should be sorry to prejudice any one against the H. house — which I might perhaps say is not the H. house at all; I hardly like to compare it to a whited sepulchre, though that simile did occur to my mind. Very fair in its exterior it was, with much plate glass, and ground glass, and gilding of letters, and shining of brass. It had been two dwelling-houses; it was now one select family hotel. But the two dwelling-houses had never been completely merged into one; never married, but joined, like the Siamese twins. There was a confusing double stairway; having ascended the right one, you were morally certain to descend the wrong. There was a confusing double hall, with doors in every direction opening everywhere but upon the way you desired to go. We mounted to the top of the house, followed by two porters with our luggage, one chambermaid with the key, another to ask if we would dine, and two more bearing large tin cans of hot water. We grew confused, and gasped, "We — we believe we don't care for any more at present, thank you," and so dismissed them all. The furniture was so out of proportion to the room that I think it must have been introduced in an infant state, and grown to its present proportions there. The one window was so high that we were obliged to jump up to look out over the mirror upon the bureau — a gymnastic feat we did not care to repeat. The bed curtains were gray; indeed there was a gray chill through the whole place. We sat down to hold a council of war. We resolved ourselves into a committee of ways and means, our feet upon the cans of hot water. "Pleasant," I said, as a leading remark, my heart beginnnig to warm under the influence of the hot water. "Pleasant?" repeated Mrs. K.; "it's enough to make one homesick. We can't stay here." "But," I interposed, "suppose we leave here, and can't get in anywhere else?" A vision of the Babes in the Wood rose before me. There was a rap at the door; the fourth chambermaid, to announce dinner. We finished our consultation hurriedly, and descended to the parlor, where we were to dine. It was a small room, already occupied by a large table and a party from the country; an old lady to play propriety, a middle-aged person of severe countenance to act it, and a pair of incipient and insipid lovers. He was a spectacled prig in a white necktie, a clergyman, I suppose, though he looked amazingly like a waiter, and she a little round combination of dimples and giggle.

He. "Have you been out for a walk this morning?"

She. "No; te-he-he-he."

He. "You ought to, you know."

She. "Te-he-he-he — yes."

He. "You should always exercise before dinner."

She. "Te-he-he-he."

Here the words gave out entirely, and, it being remarkably droll, all joined in the chorus. "We must go somewhere else, if possible," we explained to Mrs. B., when, a little later, we found our way to her door. "At least we shall be better contented if we make the attempt." The Good Man offered his protection; we found a cab, and proceeded to explore the city, asking admittance in vain at one hotel after another, until at last the Golden Cross upon the Strand, more charitable than its neighbor, or less full, opened its doors, and the good landlady, of unbounded proportions, made us both welcome and comfortable. Quite palatial did our neat bed-room, draped in white, appear. We were the proud possessors, also, of a parlor, with a round mirror over the mantel, a round table in the centre, a sofa, of which Pharaoh's heart is no comparison as regards hardness, a row of stiff, proper arm-chairs, and any amount of ornamentation in the way of works of art upon the walls, and shining snuffers and candlesticks upon the mantel. Our bargain completed, there remained nothing to be done but to remove our baggage from the other house, which I am sure we could never have attempted alone. Think of walking in and addressing the landlady, while the chambermaids and waiters peeped from behind the doors, with, "We don't like your house, madam. Your rooms are tucked up, your beds uninviting, your chambermaids frowsy, your waiters stupid, and your little parlor an abomination." How could we have done it? The Good Man volunteered. "But do you not mind?" "Not in the least." Is it not wonderful? How can we believe in the equality of the sexes? In less than an hour we were temporarily settled in our new quarters, our rescued trunks consigned to the little bed-room, our heart-felt gratitude in the possession of the Good Man.

We took our meals now in our own parlor, trying the solitary confinement system of the English during our two days' stay. It seemed a month. Not a sign of life was there, save the landlady's pleasant face behind the bar and the waiter who answered our bell, with the exception of a pair of mammoth shoes before the next door, mornings, and the bearded face of a man that startled us, once, upon the stairs. And yet the house was full. It was a relief when our two days of banishment were over, when in Mrs. B.'s pretty drawing-room, and around her table, we could again meet friends, and realize that we were still in the world.

CHAPTER III.

EXCURSIONS FROM LONDON.

Strange ways. — "The bears that went over to Charlestown." — The delights of a runaway without its dangers. — Flower show at the Crystal Palace. — Whit-Monday at Hampton Court. — A queen baby. — "But the carpets?" — Poor Nell Gwynne. — Vandyck faces. — Royal beds. — Lunch at the King's Arms. — O Music, how many murders have been committed in thy name! — Queen Victoria's home at Windsor. — A new "house that Jack built." — The Round Tower. — Stoke Pogis. — Frogmore. — The Knights of the Garter. — The queen's gallery. — The queen's plate. — The royal mews. — The wicker baby-wagons. — The state equipages.

WE bought an umbrella, — every one buys an umbrella who goes to London, — and this, in its alpaca glory, became our constant companion. We purchased a guide-book to complete our equipments; but so disreputable, so yellow-covered, was its outward appearance, so suggestive of everything but facts, that we consigned it to oblivion, and put ourselves under the guidance of our Boston friends, the Good Man and his family.

For two busy weeks we rattled over the flat pavings of the city in the low, one-horse cabs. We climbed towers, we descended into crypts, we examined tombstones, we gazed upon mummies. Everything was new, strange, and wonderful, even to the little boys in the street, who, as well as the omnibus drivers, were decked out in tall silk hats — a piece of absurdity in one case, and extravagance in the other, to our minds. The one-horse carriages rolled about upon two wheels; the occupants, like cross children, facing in every direction but the one they were going, and everybody, contrary to all our preconceived ideas of law and order, turned to the left, instead of to the right, — to say nothing of other strange and perplexing ways that came under our observation. We had come abroad upon the same errand as the bears who "went over to Charlestown to see what they could see," and so stared into every window, into every passing face, as though we were seeking the lost. We became known as the women who wanted a cab; our appearance within the iron posts that guard the entrance to Queen's Square from Southampton Row being the signal for a perfect Babel of unintelligible shouts and gesticulations down the long line of waiting vehicles, with the charging down upon us of the first half dozen in a highly dangerous manner. Wisdom is sometimes the growth of days; and we soon learned to dart out in an unexpected moment, utterly deaf and blind to everything and everybody but the first man and the first horse, and thus to go off in triumph.

But if our exit was triumphant, what was our entry to the square, when weary, faint with seeing, hearing, and trying in vain to fix everything seen and heard in our minds, we returned in a hansom! English ladies do not much affect this mode of conveyance, but American women abroad have, or take, a wide margin in matters of mere conventionality,—and so ride in hansom cabs at will. They are grown-up baby perambulators upon two wheels; the driver sitting up behind, where the handle would be, and drawing the reins of interminable length over the top of the vehicle. Picture it in your mind, and then wonder, as I did, what power of attraction keeps the horse upon the ground; what prevents his flying into the air when the driver settles down into his seat. A pair of low, folding doors take the place of a lap robe; you dash through the street at an alarming rate without any visible guide, experiencing all the delights of a runaway without any of its dangers.

FLOWER SHOW AT THE CRYSTAL PALACE.

A ride by rail of half an hour takes one to Sydenham. It is a charming walk from the station through the tastefully arranged grounds, with their shrubberies, roseries, and fountains, along the pebble-strewn paths, crowded this day with visitors. The palace itself is so like its familiar pictures as to need no description. Much of the grandeur of its vast proportions within is lost by its divisions and subdivisions. There are courts representing the various nations of the earth,— America, as usual, felicitously and truthfully shown up by a pair of scantily attired savages under a palm tree; there are the courts of the Alhambra, of Nineveh, and of Pompeii; there are fountains, and statues, and bazaars innumerable, where one may purchase almost anything as a souvenir; there are cafés where one may refresh the body, and an immense concert hall where one may delight the soul,—and how much more I cannot tell, for the crowd was almost beyond belief, and a much more interesting study than Egyptian remains, or even the exquisite mass of perfumed bloom, that made the air like summer, and the whole place a garden. They were of the English middle class, the upper middle class, bordering upon the nobility,—these rotund, fine-looking gentlemen in white vests and irreproachable broadcloth, these stout, red-faced, richly-attired ladies, with their soft-eyed, angular daughters following in their train, or clinging to their arms. We listened for an hour to the queen's own band in scarlet and gold, and then came back to town, meeting train after train filled to overflowing with expensively arrayed humanity in white kids, going out for the evening.

A DAY AT HAMPTON COURT.

It was Whit-Monday,—the workingman's holiday,—a day of sun and shower; but we took our turn upon the outside of the private omnibus chartered for the occasion, unmindful of the drops; our propelling power, six gray horses. By virtue of this private establishment we were free to pass through Hyde Park,—that breathing-place of aristocracy, where no public vehicle, no servant without livery, is tolerated. It was early, and only the countless hoof prints upon Rotten Row suggested the crowd of wealth and fashion that would throng here later in the day. One solitary equestrian there was; perched upon a guarded saddle, held in her place by some concealed band, serenely content, rode a queen baby in long, white robes. A groom led the little pony. She looked at us in grave wonder as we dashed by,— born to the purple! I cannot begin to describe to you the rising up of London for this day of pleasure; the decking of itself out in holiday attire; the garnishing of itself with paper flowers; the smooth, hard roads leading into the country, all alive; the drinking, noisy crowd about the door of every pot-house along the way. It was a delightful drive of a dozen or more miles, through the most charming suburbs imaginable,— past lawns, and gardens, and green old **trees shading** miniature parks; past "detached" villas that had **blossomed** into windows; indeed, the plate glass upon houses of most modest pretension was almost reckless extravagance in our eyes, forgetting, as we did, the slight duty **to be paid** here **upon what** is, with us, an expensive luxury. No wonder the English are a healthful people,— the sun shines upon them. I like their manner of house-building, of home-making. They set up first a great bay-window, **with a room behind** it, which is of secondary importance, with wide steps leading up to a door at the side. They fill this window with the rarest, rosiest, most rollicksome flowers. Then, if there remain time, and space, and means, other rooms **are** added, the bay-windows increasing **in direct proportion**; while shades, drawn shades, are a **thing** unknown. "But the carpets?" They are so **foolish** as to value health **above carpets**.

It was high noon when we rolled up the wide avenue of Bushey Park, with its double border of gigantic chestnuts and limes, through Richmond Park, with its vast sweep of greensward flecked with the sunbeams, dripping like the rain through the royal oaks, past Richmond terrace, with its fine residences looking out upon the Thames, the translucent stream, pure and beautiful here, before going down to the city to be defiled — like many a life. We dismounted at the gates to the palace, in the rambling old village that clings to its skirts, and joined the crowd passing through its wide portals.

It is an old palace thrown aside, given over to poor relatives, by royalty, — as we throw aside an old gown; a vast pile of dingy, red brick that has straggled over acres of Hampton parish, and is kept within bounds by a high wall of the same ugly material. It has pushed itself up into towers and turrets, with pinnacles and spires rising from its battlemented walls. It has thrust itself out into oriel and queer little latticed windows that peep into the gardens and overhang the three quadrangles, and is with its vast gardens and park, with its wide canal and avenues of green old trees, the most delightfully ugly, old place imaginable. Here kings and queens have lived and loved, suffered and died, from Cardinal Wolsey's time down to the days of Queen Anne. It is now one of England's show places; one portion of its vast extent, with the grounds, being thrown open to the public, the remainder given to decayed nobility, or wandering, homeless representatives of royalty, — a kind of royal almshouse, in fact. A curtained window, the flutter of a white hand, were to us the only signs of inhabitation.

Through thirty or more narrow, dark, bare rooms, — bare but for the pictures that crowded the walls, — we wandered. There were two or three halls of stately proportions finely decorated with frescoes by Verrio, and one or two royal stairways, up and down which slippered feet have passed, silken skirts trailed, and heavy hearts been carried, in days gone by. The pictures are mostly portraits of brave men and lovely women, of kings and queens and royal favorites,—poor Nell Gwynne among them, who began life by selling oranges in a theatre, and ended it by selling virtue in a palace. The Vandyck faces are wonderfully beautiful. They gaze upon you through a mist, a golden haze,—like that which hangs over the hills in the Indian summer,—from out deep, spiritual eyes; a dream of fair women they are.

There were one or two royal beds, where uneasy have lain the heads that wore a crown, and half a dozen chairs worked in tapestry by royal fingers,—whether preserved for their questionable beauty, or because of the rarity of royal industry, I do not know. We wandered through the shrubberies, paid a penny to see the largest grape vine in the world,—and wished we had given it to the heathen, so like its less distinguished sisters did the vine appear,—and at last lunched at the King's Arms, a queer little inn just outside the gates, edging our way with some difficulty through the noisy, guzzling crowd around the door—the crowd that, having reached the acme of the day's felicity, was fast degenerating into a quarrel. In the long, bare room at the head of the narrow, winding stairs, we found comparative quiet. The tables were covered with joints of beef, with loaves of bread, pitchers of ale, and the ubiquitous cheese. A red-faced young man in tight new clothes—like a strait-jacket—occupied one end of our table with his blushing sweetheart. A band of wandering harpers harped upon their harps to the crowd of wrangling men and blowsy women in the open court below; strangely out of tune were the harps, out of time the measure, according well with the spirit of the hour. A loud-voiced girl decked out in tawdry finery, with face like solid brass, sang "Annie Laurie" in hard, metallic tones, — O Music, how many murders have been committed in thy name! — then passed a cup for pennies, with many a jest and rude, bold laugh. We were glad when the day was done, — glad when we had turned away from it all.

QUEEN VICTORIA'S HOME AT WINDSOR.

The castle itself is a huge, battlemented structure of gray stone, — a fortress as well as a palace, — with a home park of five hundred acres, the private grounds of Mrs. Guelph, and, beyond that, a grand park of eighteen hundred acres. But do not imagine that she lives here with only her children and servants about her, — this kindly German widow, whose throne was once in the hearts of her people. Royalty is a complicated affair, — a wheel within a wheel, — and reminds us of nothing so much as "the house that Jack built."

This is the Castle of Windsor.

This is the queen that lives in the Castle of Windsor.

These are the ladies that 'tend on the queen that lives in the Castle of Windsor.

These are the pages that bow to the ladies that 'tend on the queen that lives in the Castle of Windsor.

These are the lackeys that wait on the pages that bow to the ladies that 'tend on the queen that lives in the Castle of Windsor.

These are the soldiers, tried and sworn, that guard the crown from the unicorn, that stand by the lackeys that wait on the pages that bow to the ladies that 'tend on the queen that lives in the Castle of Windsor.

These are the "military knights" forlorn, founded by Edward before you were born, that outrank the soldiers, tried and sworn, that guard the crown from the unicorn, that stand by the lackeys that wait on the pages that bow to the ladies that 'tend on the queen that lives in the Castle of Windsor.

These are the knights that the garter have worn, with armorial banners tattered and torn, that look down on the military knights forlorn, founded by Edward before you were born, that outrank the soldiers, tried and sworn, that guard the crown from the unicorn, that stand by the lackeys that wait on the pages that bow to the ladies that 'tend on the queen that lives in the Castle of Windsor.

This is the dean, all shaven and shorn, with the canons and clerks that doze in the morn, that install the knights that the garter have worn, with armorial banners tattered and torn, that look down on the military knights forlorn, founded by Edward before you were born, that outrank the soldiers, tried and sworn, that guard the crown from the unicorn, that stand by the lackeys that wait on the pages that bow to the ladies that 'tend on the queen that lives in the Castle of Windsor.

And so on. The train within the castle walls that follows the queen is endless.

We passed through the great, grand, state apartments, refurnished at the time of the marriage of the

Prince of Wales, for the use of the Danish family. We mounted to the battlements of the Round Tower by the hundred steps, the grim cannon gazing down upon us from the top. Half a dozen visitors were already there, gathered as closely as possible about the angular guide, listening to his geography lesson, and looking off upon the wonderful panorama of park, and wood, and winding river. Away to the right rose the spire of Stoke Pogis Church, where the curfew still "tolls the knell of parting day." To the left, in the great park below, lay Frogmore, where sleeps Prince Albert the Good. Eton College, too, peeped out from among the trees, its gardens touching the Thames, and in the distance, — beyond the sleeping villages tucked in among the trees, — the shadowy blue hills held up the sky.

St. George's Chapel is in the quadrangle below. It is the chapel of the Knights of the Garter. And now, when you read of the chapels, or churches, or cathedrals in the old world, — and they are all in a sense alike, — pray don't imagine a New England meeting-house with a double row of stiff pews and a choir in the gallery singing "Antioch"! The body of the chapel was a great, bare space, with tablets and elaborate monuments against the walls. Opening from this were alcoves, — also called chapels, — each one containing the tombs and monuments of some family. As many of the inscriptions are dated centuries back, you can imagine they are often quaintly expressed. One old knight, who died in Catholic times, desired an open Breviary to remain always in the niche before his tomb, that passers might read to their comfort, and say for him an orison.

Of course this would never do in the days when the chapel fell into Protestant hands. A Bible was substituted, chained into its place; but the old inscription, cut deep in the stone, still remains, beginning "Who leyde thys book here?" with a startling appropriateness of which the author never dreamed. Over another of these chapels is rudely cut an ox, an N, and a bow, — the owner having, in an antic manner, hardly befitting the place, thus written his name — Oxenbow.

You enter the choir, where the installations take place, by steps, passing under the organ. In the chancel is a fine memorial window to Prince Albert. On either side are the stalls or seats for the knights, with the armorial banner of each hanging over his place. Projecting over the chancel, upon one side, is what appears to be a bay-window. This is the queen's gallery, a little room with blue silk hangings, — for blue is the color worn by Knights of the Garter, — where she sits during the service. Through these curtains she looked down upon the marriage of the Prince of Wales. Think of being thus put away from everybody, as though one were plague-stricken. A private station awaits her when she steps from the train at the castle gates. A private room is attached to the green-houses, to the riding-school in the park, and even to the private chapel. A private photograph-room, for the taking of the royal pictures, adjoins her apartments. It must be a fine thing to be a queen, — and so tiresome! Even the gold spoon in one's mouth could not offset the weariness of it all, and of gold spoons she has an unbounded supply; from ten to fifteen millions of dollars worth of gold plate for her majesty's table being guarded within the castle! Think of it, little women who set up house-keeping with half a dozen silver tea-spoons and a salt-spoon!

We waited before a great gate until the striking of some forgotten hour, to visit the royal mews. You may walk through all these stables in slippers and in your daintiest gown, without fear. A stiff young man in black — a cross between an undertaker and an incipient clergyman in manner — acted as guide. Other parties, led by other stiff young men, followed or crossed our path. There were stalls and stalls, upon either side, in room after room, — for one could not think of calling them stables, — filled by sleek bays for carriage or saddle. And the ponies! — the dear little shaggy browns, with sweeping tails, and wonderful eyes peeping out from beneath moppy manes, the milk-white, tiny steeds, with hair like softest silk, — they won our hearts. Curled up on the back of one, fast asleep, lay a Maltese kitten; the "royal mew" some one called it. The carriages were all plain and dark, for the ordinary use of the court. In one corner a prim row of little yellow, wicker, baby-wagons attracted our attention, like those used by the poorest mother in the land. In these the royal babies have taken their first airings.

The state equipages we saw another day at Buckingham Palace, — the cream-colored horses, the carriages and harnesses all crimson and gold. There they stand, weeks and months together, waiting for an occasion. The effect upon a fine day, under favoring auspices, — the sun shining, the bands playing, the crowd of gazers, the prancing horses, the gilded chariots, — must almost equal the triumphal entry of a first class circus into a New England town!

CHAPTER IV.

SIGHT-SEEING IN LONDON.

The Tower. — The tall Yankee of inquiring mind. — Our guide in gorgeous array. — War trophies. — Knights in armor. — A professional joke. — The crown jewels. — The house where the little princes were smothered. — The " Traitor's Gate."— The Houses of Parliament. — What a throne is like. — The "woolsack." — The Peeping Gallery for ladies. — Westminster Hall and the law courts. — The three drowsy old women. — The Great Panjandrum himself. — Johnson and the pump. — St. Paul's. — Wellington's funeral car. — The Whispering Gallery. — The bell.

THE TOWER.

IT is not a tower at all, as we reckon towers, you must know, but a walled town upon the banks of the Thames, in the very heart of London. Hundreds of years ago, when what is now this great city was only moor and marsh, the Romans built here — a castle, perhaps. Only a bit of crumbling wall, of mouldering pavement, remain to tell the story. When the Normans came in to possess the land, William the Conqueror erected upon this spot a square fortress, with towers rising from its four corners. Every succeeding monarch added a castle, a tower, a moat, to strengthen its strength and extend its limits, until, in time, it covered twelve acres of land, as it does to this day. Here the kings and queens of England lived in comfortless state, until the time of Queen Elizabeth, having need to be hedged about with something more than royalty to insure safety. Times have changed; swords have been beaten into ploughshares; and where the moat once encircled the tower wall, flowers blossom now. The dungeons that for centuries held prisoners of state do not confine any one to-day; and the strongholds that guarded the person of England's sovereign keep in safety now the jewels and the crown. There are round towers, and square towers, and, for anything I know, three-cornered towers, each with its own history of horrors. There are windows from which people were thrown, bridges over which they were dragged, and dark holes in which they were incarcerated.

To appreciate all this, you should see it — as we did one chilly May morning. We huddled about the stove in the waiting-room upon the site of the old royal menagerie, our companions a round man, with a limp gingham cravat and shabby coat, a little old woman in a poke bonnet, and half a dozen or more school-boys from the country. A tall Yankee of inquiring mind joined us as we sallied from the door, led by a guide gorgeous in ruff and buckles, cotton velvet and gilt lace, and with all these glories surmounted by a black hat, that swelled out at the top in a wonderful manner. Down the narrow street within the gates, over the slippery cobble-stones, under considerable mental excitement, and our alpaca umbrella, we followed our guide to an archway, before which he paused, and struck an attitude. The long Yankee darted forward. "Stand back, my friends, stand back," said the

"A dozen umbrellas were tipped up; the rain fell fast upon a dozen upturned, expectant faces." Page 57.

guide. "You will please form a circle." Immediately a dozen umbrellas surrounded him. He pointed to a narrow window over our heads; a dozen umbrellas were tipped up; the rain fell fast upon a dozen upturned, expectant faces. "In that room, Sir ——" (I could not catch the name) "spent the night before his execution, in solemn meditation and prayer." There was a circular groan of sympathy and approval from a dozen lips, the re-cant of a dozen dripping umbrellas, and we pattered on to the next point of interest, following our leader through pools of blood, figuratively speaking, — literally, through pools of water, — our eyes distended, our cheeks pale with horror. Ah, what treasures of credulity we must have been to the guides in those days! Time brought unbelief and hardness of heart.

We mounted stairs narrow and dark; we descended stairs dark and narrow; we entered chambers gloomy and grim. The half I could not tell — of the rooms filled with war trophies — scalps in the belt of the nation — from the Spanish Armada down to the Sepoy rebellion; the long hall, with its double row of lumbering old warriors encased in steel, as though they had stepped into a steel tower and walked off, tower and all, some fine morning; the armory, with its stacked arms for thirty thousand men. "We may have occasion to use them," said the guide, facetiously, making some reference to the speech of Mr. Sumner, just then acting the part of a stick to stir up the British lion. The Yankee chuckled complacently, and we, too, refused to quake. There was a room filled with instruments of torture, diabolical inventions, recalling the days of the Inquisition. The Yankee expressed a desire to "see how some o' them things worked." Opening from this was an unlighted apartment, with walls of stone, a dungeon indeed, in which we were made to believe that Sir Walter Raleigh spent twelve years of his life. No shadow of doubt would have fallen upon our unquestioning minds, had we been told that he amused himself during this time by standing upon his head. "Walk in, walk in," said the smiling guide, as we peered into its darkness. We obeyed. "Now," said he, "that you may appreciate his situation, I will step out and close the door." The little old woman screamed; the Yankee made one stride to the opening; the guide laughed. It was only a professional joke; there was no door. We saw the bare prison-room, with its rough fireplace, the slits between the stones of the wall to admit light and air, and the initials of Lady Jane Grey, with a host more of forgotten names, upon the walls. Just outside, within the quadrangle, where the grass grew green beneath the summer rain, she was beheaded,—poor little innocent,—who had no desire to be a queen! In another tower close by, guarded by iron bars, were the royal jewels and the crown, for which all this blood was shed — pretty baubles of gold and precious stones, but hardly worth so many lives.

You remember the story of the princes smothered in the Tower by command of their cruel uncle? There was the narrow passage in the wall where the murderers came at night; the worn step by which they entered the great, bare room where the little victims slept; the winding stairs down which the bodies were thrown. Beneath the great stone at the foot they were secretly buried. Then the stairway was walled up, lest the stones should cry out; and no one knew the story of the burial until long, long afterwards — only a few years since — when the walled-up stairway was discovered, the stones at the foot displaced, and a heap of dust, of little crumbling bones, revealed it. A rosy-faced, motherly woman, the wife of a soldier quartered in the barracks here, answered the rap of the guide upon the nail-studded door opening from one of the courts, and told us the old story. "The bed of the princes stood just there," she said, pointing to one corner, where, by a curious coincidence, a little bed was standing now. She answered the question in our eyes with, "My boys sleep there." But do you not fear that the murderers will come back some night by this same winding way, and smother them?" How she laughed! And, indeed, what had ghosts to do with such a cheery body!

Down through the "Traitors' Gate," with its spiked portcullis, we could see the steps leading to the water. Through this gate prisoners were brought from trial at Westminster. It is said that the Princess Elizabeth was dragged up here when she refused to come of her own will, knowing too well that they who entered here left hope behind. A little later, with music and the waving of banners, and amid the shouts of the people, she rode out of the great gates into the city, the Queen of England.

THE HOUSES OF PARLIAMENT.

Though they have stood barely thirty years, already the soft gray limestone begins to crumble away, — the elements, with a sense of the fitness of things, striving to act the part of time, and bring them into a likeness of the adjoining abbey. There is an exquisite beauty in the thousand gilded points and pinnacles that pierce the fog, or shine softly through the mist that veils the city. Ethereal, shadowy, unreal they are, like the spires of a celestial city, or the far away towers and turrets we see sometimes at sunset in the western sky.

Here, you know, are the chambers of the Houses of Lords and Commons, with the attendant lobbies, libraries, committee-rooms, &c., and a withdrawing-room for the use of the queen when she is graciously pleased to open Parliament in person. The speaker of the House of Commons, as well as some other officials, reside here — a novel idea to us, who could hardly imagine the speaker of our House of Representatives taking up his abode in the Capitol! Parliament was not in session, and we walked through the various rooms at will, even to the robing-room of the noble lords, where the peg upon which Lord Stanley hangs his hat was pointed out; and very like other pegs it was. At one end of the chamber of the House of Lords is the throne. It is a simple affair enough — a gilded arm-chair on a little platform reached by two or three steps, and with crimson hangings. Extending down on either side are the crimson-cushioned seats without desks. In the centre is a large square ottoman, — the woolsack, — which might, with equal appropriateness, be called almost anything else. Above, a narrow gallery offers a lounging-place to the sons and friends of the peers; and at one end, above the throne, is a high loft, a kind of uplifted amen corner, for strangers, with a space where women may sit and look down through a screen of lattice-work upon the proceedings below. It seems a remnant of Eastern customs, strangely out of place in this Western world, and akin to the shrouding of ourselves in veils, like our Oriental sisters. Or can it be that the noble lords are more keenly sensitive to the distracting influence of bright eyes than other men?

WESTMINSTER HALL AND THE LAW COURTS.

Adjoining the Houses of Parliament is this vast old hall. For almost five hundred years has it stood, its curiously carved roof unsupported by column or pillar. Here royal banquets, as well as Parliaments, have been held, and more than one court of justice. Here was the great trial of Warren Hastings. It was empty now of everything but echoes and the long line of statuary on either side, except the lawyers in their long, black gowns, who hastened up and down its length, or darted in and out the three baize doors upon one side, opening into the Courts of Chancery, Common Pleas, and the Exchequer. Our national curiosity was aroused, and we mounted the steps to the second, which had won our sympathies from its democratic name.

There were high, straight-backed pews of familiar appearance, rising one above the other, into the last of which we climbed, a certain Sunday solemnity stealing over us, a certain awkward consciousness that we were the observed of all observers, since we were the only spectators — a delusion of our vanity, however. In the high gallery before us, in complacent comfort, sat three fat, drowsy old women (?) in white, curling wigs, and voluminous gowns, asking all manner of distracting questions, and requiring to be told over and over again, — after the manner of drowsy old women, — to the utter confusion of a poor witness in the front pew, who clung to the rail and swayed about hopelessly, while he tried to tell his story, as if by this rotary motion he could churn his ideas into form. Not only did he lose the thread of his discourse, — he became hopelessly entangled in it. Scratch, scratch, scratch, went the pens all around him. Every word, as it fell from his lips, was pounced upon by the begowned, bewigged, bewildering judges, was twisted and turned by the lawyers, was tossed back and forth throughout the court-room, until there arose a question in our minds, as to who was telling the story. All the while the lawyers were glaring upon him as though he was perjuring himself with every word — as who would not be, under the circumstances? And such lawyers! They dotted the pews all around us. The long, black gowns were not so bad; they hid a deal of awkwardness, I doubt not. But the wigs! the queer little curly things, perched upon every head, and worn with such a perverse delight in misfits! the small men being invariably hidden beneath the big wigs, and the large men strutting about like the great Panjandrum himself with the little round button at the top! The appearance of one, whose head, through some uncommon development, rose to a ridge-pole behind, was surprising, to say the least. It was not alone that his wig was too small, that a fringe of straight, black hair fell below its entire white circumference; it was not alone that it was parted upon the wrong side, or that, being mansard in form, and his head hip-roofed, it could never, by any process, have been shaped thereto; but I doubt if the wearing of it upside down, added to all these little drawbacks, could conduce to the beauty or dignity of any man. Unmindful of this reversed order of nature, its happy possessor skipped about the court-room, nodding to his brethren with a blithesome air, to the imminent peril of his top-knot, which sustained about the same relation to his head as the sword to that of Damocles. He speered down upon the poor witness. He pretended to make notes of dreadful import with a screaming quill, and, in fact, comported himself with an airy unconsciousness delightful to see.

In regard to the proceedings of the court, I only know that the point under discussion concerned one Johnson, and a pump; and Mr. Pickwick's judge sat upon the bench. Whether he was originally round, red-faced, with gooseberry eyes, I do not remember; but all these pleasing characteristics he possessed at this present time, as well as a pudgy forefinger, with which to point his remarks.

"You say," he repeated, with a solemnity of which my pen is incapable, and impressing every word upon the poor man in the front pew with this same forefinger, "that — Bunsen — went — to — the — pump?"

"Johnson, my lord," the witness ventured to correct him, in a low tone.

"It makes no difference," responded the judge, irate, "whether it is Bunsen or Jillson. The question is, Did — Jillson — go — to — the — pump?"

Whom the gods destroy they first deprive of their five senses. Four, at least, of the poor man's had departed some time since. The fifth followed. "Johnson went, my lord," he replied, doggedly. Having found one point upon which his mind was clear, he clung to it with the tenacity of despair.

"Johnson! who's *Johnson?*" gasped the bewildered judge, over whose face a net of perplexed lines spread itself upon the introduction of this new character. In the confusion of denials and explanations that followed, we descended from our perch, and stole away; nor are we at all sure, to this day, as to whether Johnson did or did not really go to the pump.

ST. PAUL'S.

Imagine our surprise, one day, when admiring a pretty ribbon upon a friend, to be told that it came from St. Paul's Churchyard. Hardly the place for ribbons, one would think; but the narrow street which encircles the cathedral in the form of a bow and its string goes by this name, and contains, besides the bookstores and publishing houses, some fine "silk mercers'" establishments.

The gray surface of the grand edifice is streaked with black, as though time had beaten it with stripes, and a pall of smoke and dust covers the statues in the court before it. Consecrated ground this is, indeed. From the earliest times of the Christian religion, through all the bigotry and fanaticism of the ages that followed, down to the present time, the word of God has been proclaimed here — in weakness often, in bitterness many times that belied the spirit of its message; by a priesthood more corrupt than the people; by noble men, beyond the age in which they lived, and whom the flames of martyrdom could not appall. Under Diocletian the first church was destroyed. It was rebuilt, and destroyed again by the Saxons. Twice has it been levelled to the ground by fire. But neither sword nor flame could subdue it, and firm as a rock it stands to-day, as it has stood for nearly two hundred years, and as it seems likely to stand for ages to come. The sacred stillness that invests the place was rudely broken, the morning of our visit, by the blows from the hammers of the workmen, resounding through the dome like a discharge of artillery. A great stage, and seats in the form of an amphitheatre, were being erected in the nave for a children's festival, which prevented our doing more than glance down its length. We read some of the inscriptions upon the monuments, that one, so often quoted, of Sir Christopher Wren, among them — "Do you seek his monument? Look around you;" glanced into the choir, with its Gothic stalls, where the service is performed, and then descended into the crypt beneath all this, that labyrinth of damp darkness where so many lie entombed. Here is the funeral car of Wellington, with candles burning around it, cast from the conquering cannon which thundered victory to a nation, but sorrow and death to many a home. Shrouded with velvet it is, as are the horses, in imitation of those which bore him to his rest. All around were marble effigies, blackened, broken, as they survived the burning of the late cathedral, at the time of the great fire. Tombstones formed the pavement. "Whose can this be?" I said, trying to follow with the point of my umbrella the half-worn inscription beneath my feet. It was that of Sir Joshua Reynolds. Strange enough it seemed to us, coming from a country so new as to have been by no means prolific in great men, to find them here lying about under our feet.

Having explored the crypt, we prepared to mount the endless winding stairs, whose final termination is the ball under the cross that surmounts the whole. Our ambition aimed only at the bell beneath the ball. We paid an occasional sixpence for the privilege of peeping into the library, — a most tidy and put-to-rights room, with a floor of wood patchwork, — and for the right to look down upon the geometrical staircase which winds around and clings to the wall upon one side, but is without any visible support upon the other. The "whispering gallery" was reached after a time. It is the encircling cornice within the dome, surrounded by a railing, and forming a narrow gallery. "I will remain here," said the guide, "while you pass around until you are exactly opposite; wait there until I whisper." Had we possessed the spirit of Casabianca, we should at this moment be sitting upon that narrow bench against the wall, with our feet upon the gas-pipes. We waited and listened, and listened and waited; but the sound of the blows from the hammers below reverberated like thunder around us. We could not have heard the crack of doom. Becoming conscious, after a time, that our guide had disappeared, we came out and continued our ascent. Mrs. K.'s curiosity, if not satisfied, was at least quenched, and she refused to go farther. My aspirations still pointed upward. There was another sixpence, another dizzy mount of dark, twisting stairs, with strength, ambition, and even curiosity gradually left behind, and with only one blind instinct remaining — to go on. There was a long, dingy passage, through which ghostly forms were flitting; there were more stairs, with twists and turns, forgotten now with other torments; there was the mounting of half a dozen rickety wooden steps at last, for no object but to descend shakily upon the other side, and then we found ourselves in a little dark corner, peering over a dingy rail, with a great, dusky object filling all the space below. And that was the bell! "Well, and what of it?" I don't know; but we saw it!

CHAPTER V.

AWAY TO PARIS.

The wedding party. — The canals. — New Haven. — Around the tea-table. — Separating the sheep from the goats. — "Will it be a rough passage?" — Gymnastic feats of the little steamer. — O, what were officers to us? — "Who ever invented earrings!" — Dieppe. — Fish-wives. — Train for Paris. — Fellow-passengers. — Rouen. — Babel. — Deliverance.

IT was the last week in May, and by no means the "merry, merry month of May" had we found it. Not only was the sky weighed down with clouds, but they dripped upon the earth continually, the sun showing his ghastly, white, half-drowned face for a moment only to be swept from sight again by the cloud waves. A friend was going to Paris. Would we shake the drops from our garments, close our umbrellas, and go with him? We not only would, we did. We gathered a lunch, packed our trunk, said our adieus, and drove down to the station in the usual pouring rain, the tearful accompaniment to all our movements. But one party besides our own awaited the train upon the platform — a young man with the insignia of bliss in the gloves of startling whiteness upon his hands, and a middle-aged woman of seraphic expression of countenance, clad in robes of spotless white, her feet encased in capacious white slippers. In this airy costume, one hand grasping a huge bouquet devoid of color, the other the arm of her companion, she paced back and forth, to the great amusement of the laughing porters, casting upon us less fortunate ones, who shivered meekly in our wraps, glances of triumphant pity indescribable.

"Weddin' party, zur," explained the guard, touching his cap to our friend. "Jus' come down in fly." They looked to us a good deal more as if they were just going up in a "fly." The train shrieked into the station, and we were soon rushing over the road to New Haven, from which, in an evil moment, we had planned to cross the Channel. There was little new or strange in the picture seen from our window. The cottages were now of a dull, clay color, instead of the dingy red we had observed before, as though they had been erected in sudden need, without waiting for the burning of the bricks. There were brick-yards all along the way, answering a vexed question in my mind as to where all the bricks came from which were used so entirely in town and village here, in the absence of the wood so plentiful with us. The canals added much to the beauty of the landscape, winding through the meadows as if they were going to no particular place, and were in no haste to reach their destination. They turned aside for a clump of willows or a mound of daisy-crowned earth; they went quite out of their way to peep into the back doors of a village, and, in fact, strolled along in a lazy, serpentine manner that would have crazed the proprietor of a Yankee canal boat.

It was five o'clock when we reached New Haven, having dropped our fellow-passengers along the way, the blissful couple among them. Through some error in calculation we had taken an earlier train than we need have, and found hours of doleful leisure awaiting us in this sleepy little town, lying upon an arm of the sea. Its outer appearance was not inviting. Here were the first and last houses of wood we saw in England, — high, ugly things, that might have been built of old boats or drift wood, with an economy that precluded all thought of grace in architecture. The train, in a gracious spirit of accommodation, instead of plunging into the sea, as it might have done, paused before the door of a hotel upon the wharf. There, in a little parlor, we improvised a home for a time. Our friend went off to explore the town. We took possession of the faded red arm-chairs by the wide windows. Down below, beyond the wet platform, rose the well-colored meerschaum of the little French steamer, whose long-boats hung just above the edge of the wharf. Through the closed window stole the breath of the salt sea, that, only a hand-breadth here, widened out below into boundlessness, bringing visions of the ocean and a thrill of remembered delight. The rain had ceased. The breeze rolled the clouds into snow-balls, pure white against the blue of the sky. Over the narrow stream came the twitter of birds, hidden in the hawthorn hedge all abloom. Everything smiled, and beamed, and glistened without, though far out to sea the white caps crowned the dancing waves. When night fell, and the lights glimmered all through the town, we drew the heavy curtains, lighted the candles in the shining candlesticks, whose light cast a delusive glow over the dingy dustiness of the room, bringing out cheerfully the little round tea-table in the centre, with its bright silver and steaming urn, over which we lingered a long hour, measuring and weighing our comfort, telling tales, seeing visions, and dreaming dreams of home.

The clock struck nine as we crossed the plank to the Alexandra, trying in vain to find in its toy appointments some likeness to our ocean steamer of delightful memory. The train whizzed in from London, bringing our fellow-voyagers. The sheep were separated from the goats by the officer at the foot of the plank, who asked each one descending, "First or second cabin?" — sending one to the right, the other to the left. The wind swept in from the sea raw and cold. The foot-square deck was cheerless and wet. Even a diagonal promenade proved short and unsatisfactory, and in despair we descended the slippery, perpendicular stairs between boxes and bales, and down still another flight, to the cabin. A narrow, cushioned seat clung to its four sides, divided into lengths for berths. "Will it be a rough night?" we carelessly asked the young stewardess. "O, no!" was the stereotyped reply, though all the while the wicked waves were dancing beneath the white caps just outside. We divested ourselves of hats, and wraps, and useless ornaments, reserving only that of a meek and quiet spirit, which, under a nameless fear, grew every moment meeker and more quiet. We undid the interminable buttons of our American boots, and prepared for a comfortable rest, with an ignorance that at the time approximated bliss. There was leisure for the working out of elaborate schemes. Something possessed the tide. Whether it was high or low, narrow or wide, I do not know; but there at the wharf we were to await the working of its own will, regardless of time. Accordingly we selected our places with a deliberation that bore no proportion to the time we were to fill them, advising with the stewardess, who had settled herself comfortably to sleep. We tried our heads to England and our feet to the foe, and then reversed the order, finally compromising by taking a position across the Channel. But the loading of the steamer overhead, with the chattering of our fellow-passengers below, — two English girls, a pretty brunette and her sister, — banished sleep. At three o'clock our voyage began — the succession of quivering leaps, plunges, and somersaults which miraculously landed us upon the French coast. I can think of no words to describe it. The first night upon the ocean was paradise and the perfection of peace in comparison. To this day the thought of the swashing water, beaten white against the port-hole before my eyes, is sickening. A calm — to me, of utter prostration — fell upon us long after the day dawned, only to be broken by the stewardess, when sleep had brought partial forgetfulness, with, "It's nine o'clock; we're at Dieppe, and the officers want to come in here." We tried to raise our heads. Officers! What officers? Had we crossed the Styx? Were they of light or darkness? We sank back. O, what were officers to us!

"But you must get up!" — and she began an awkward attempt at the buttons of those horrible boots. That recalled to life. American boots are of this world, and we made a feeble attempt to don some of its vanities. O, how senseless did the cuffs appear that went on upside down!—the collar which was fastened under **one** ear!—the ribbons that were consigned to our pockets! Making blind stabs **at our ears,** "Good heavens!" we ejaculated, "who ever invented ear-rings? Relics of barbarism!" We made hasty thrusts at the hair-pins, standing out from our heads in every direction like enraged porcupine quills; being pulled, and twisted, and scolded by the stewardess all the while; hearing the thump, thump, upon our door as one pair of knuckles after another awoke the **echoes, as one** strange voice after another shouted, "**Why don't** those ladies come out?" O the trembling fingers that refused to hold the pins!—the trembling feet that staggered up the ladder-like stairs as we were **thrust** out of the cabin—out of the cruel little steamer to take refuge in one of the waiting cabs! O the blessedness of our thick veils **and** charitable wraps!

I recall, as though it **were** a dream, the narrow, roughly-paved street of Dieppe; a latticed window filled with **flowers, and** a dark-eyed maiden peeping through the leaves; the fish-wives in short petticoats and with high white caps, clattering over the stones in their wooden *sabots,* wheeling barrows of fish to the market near **the** station, where they bartered, **and bar-**gained, and gossiped. Evidently it is a woman's right in Normandy to work—to grow as withered, and hard, **and** old before **the** time **as** she chooses, **or as** she has need; for to put away year after year, as do these poor women, every grace and charm of womanhood, cannot be of choice.

At the long table in the refreshment-room of the station we drank the tasteless tea, and ate a slice from the roll four feet in length. The English-speaking girl who attended us found a place — rough enough, to be sure — where in the few moments of waiting we could complete our hasty toilets. Beside us at the table, our fellow-voyagers, were two professors from a Connecticut college of familiar name, whom we had met in London. They joined us in the comfortable railway carriage, and added not a little to the pleasant chat that shortened the long day and the weary journey to Paris. Our number — for the compartment held eight — was completed by a young American gentleman, and a Frenchman of evil countenance, who drank wine and made love to his pretty Lizette in an unblushing manner, strange, and by no means pleasing, to us, demonstrating the annoyance, if nothing worse, to which one is often subjected in these compartment cars. It needed but one glance from the window to convince us that we were no longer in England. To be sure, the sky is blue, the grass green, in all lands; but in place of the level sweep of meadow through which we had passed across the Channel, the land swelled here into hills on every side. Long rows of stiff poplars divided the fields, or stretched away in straight avenues as far as the eye could reach. The English remember the beauty of a curved line; the French, with a painful rectitude, describe only right angles. Scarlet poppies blushed among the purple, yellow, and white wild flowers along the way. The plastered cottages with their high, thatched roofs, the tortuous River Seine with its green islands, as we neared Paris, the neat little stations along the way — like gingerbread houses — made for us a new and charming panorama. Hanging over a gate at one of these stations was an old man, white-haired, blind; his guide, an old woman, who waited, with a kind of wondering awe stealing over her withered face, while he played some simple air upon a little pipe — thus asking alms. So simple was the air, the very shadow of a melody, that the scene might have been amusing, had it not been so pitiful.

At noon we lunched in the comfortless waiting-room at Rouen, while the professors made a hasty visit to the cathedral during our stay of half an hour. We still suffered from the tossing of the sea, and cathedrals possessed no charms in our eyes. It was almost night when we reached Paris, and joined the hurrying crowd descending from the train. It was a descent into Pandemonium. There was a confusion of unintelligible sounds in our ears like the roll of a watchman's rattle, bringing no suggestion of meaning. The calmness of despair fell upon our crushed spirits, with a sense of powerlessness such as we never experienced before or since. A dim recollection of school-days — of Ollendorff — rose above the chaos in our minds. "Has the physician of the shoemaker the canary of the carpenter?" we repeated mechanically; and with that our minds became a blank.

Deliverance awaited us; and when, just outside the closed gates, first in the expectant crowd, we espied the face of a friend, peace enveloped us like a garment. Our troubles were over.

CHAPTER VI.

THE PARIS OF 1869.

The devil. — Cathedrals and churches. — The Louvre. — Modern French art. — The Beauvais clock, with its droll little puppets. — Virtue in a red gown. — The Luxembourg Palace. — The yawning statue of Marshal Ney. — Gay life by gaslight. — The Imperial Circus. — The Opera. — How the emperor and empress rode through the streets after the riots. — The beautiful Spanish woman whose face was her fortune. — Napoleon's tomb.

IT may be the City of Destruction, the very gateway to depths unknown; but with its fair, white dwellings, its fair, white streets, that gleamed almost like gold beneath a summer sun, it seemed much more a City Celestial. It may be, as some affirm, that the devil here walks abroad at midday; but we saw neither the print of his hoofs upon the asphaltum, nor the shadow of his horns upon the cream-like Caen stone. We walked, and rode, and dwelt a time within its limits; and but for a certain reckless gayety that gave to the Sabbath an air of Vanity Fair, but for the mallet of the workman that disturbed our Sunday worship, we should never have known that we were not in the most Christian of all Christian cities. It is by no means imperative to do in Rome as the Romans do, and one need not in Paris drink absinthe or visit the Jardin Mabille.

Our first expedition was to the banker's and to the shops, and having replenished our purse and wardrobe, we were prepared to besiege the city. There was a day or two of rest in the gilded chairs, cushioned with blue satin, of our pretty *salon*, whence we peeped down upon the street below between the yellow satin curtains that draped its wide French window; or rolled our eyes meditatively to the delicately tinted ceiling, with its rose-colored clouds skimmed by tiny, impossible birds; or made abortive attempts to penetrate the secrets of the buhl cabinets, and to guess at the time from the pretty clocks of disordered organism; or admired ourselves in the mirrors which gazed at each other from morning till night, for our apartments in the little Hotel Friedland we found most charming.

You will hardly care for a description of the dozen, more or less, churches, old, new, and restored, with which we began and ended our sight-seeing in Paris, where we looked upon sculptured saints without number, and studied ecclesiastical architecture to more than our hearts' content. There was St. Germain L'Auxerrois, the wicked old bell of which tolled the signal for the massacre of St. Bartholomew. We stood with the *bonnes* and babies under the trees of the square before it, gazing up at the belfry with most severe countenances, — and learned, afterwards, that the bell had been long since removed! There was the Madeleine of more recent date, built in the form of a Greek temple, and interesting just now for having been the church of Father Hyacinthe, to which we could for a time **find no** entrance. We shook the iron gate; we inquired **in** excellent English of a French shopkeeper, and found at last an open gateway, a little unlocked door, beyond which we spent a time of search and inquiry in darkness, and among wood, and shavings, and broken chairs, and holy dust-pans, **before passing** around and entering the great bronze **doors.** There were the Pantheon and St. Sulpice, grand and beautiful, erected piously from the proceeds of lotteries. There was St. Etienne du Mont, and within one of its chapels the gilded tomb of the patron saint of Paris — St. Genevieve. Who she was, or what she did to gain this rather unenviable position, I failed to learn. Her name seems to have outlived her deeds. **Whether she** was beautiful and beloved, and put away earthly vanities for a **holy** life, or old and ugly, **and** bore her lot with a patience that won saintship, I do not know. I can only tell that tapers burn always upon her tomb, and if you buy one it will burn a prayer for you. So we were told. There is one old church, St. Germain des Prés, most beautifully colored within. Its pictures seem to have melted upon the walls. But admired above all is the Sainte Chapelle, in the Palais de Justice, a chapel fitted up by the fanatical St. Louis, when this palace of justice, which holds now the courts of law, was a royal residence. Of course all its brightness was dimmed long ago. Its glories became dust, like its founder. But it has recently been restored, and **is a marvel of** gilt, well-**blended** colors, and stained glass. A graceful spire **surmounts it,** but the old, cone-capped towers, rising from another part of the same building, possessed far greater interest in our eyes; for here was the Conciergerie, where were confined Marie Antoinette and so many more victims of the reign of terror.

On the "isle of the city," in the Seine, where, under the Roman rule, a few mud huts constituted Paris, stands the church of Notre Dame, which was three hundred years in building. With its spire and two square towers, it may be seen from almost any part of the city. I wish you might look upon the relics and the vestments which the priests wear upon occasions of ceremony, hidden within this church, and displayed upon the payment of an extra fee. I did not wonder that the Sisters of Charity, who went into the little room with us, gazed aghast upon the gold and **silver**, and precious stones.

Every one visits the galleries of the Louvre, of course. A little, worn shoe, belonging once to Marie Antoinette, and the old gray coat of the first emperor, were to us the most interesting objects among the relics. From out the sea of pictures rise Murillo's Madonna, the lovely face with a soul behind it, shining through, and the burial of the heroine of Chateaubriand. Do you know it? The fair form, the sweeping hair of Attila, and the dark lover with despair in his face? As for the Rubens gallery,—his fat, red, undraped women here among the clouds, surrounded **by** puffy little cherubs, had for us no charms. Rubens in Antwerp was a revelation. We wandered through room after room, lighted from above, crowded with paintings. To live for a time among them would be a delight; **to glance** at them for a moment was tantalization. All around were the easels of the artists who come here to sketch — sharp-featured, heavy-browed men, with unkempt hair and flowing beards, and in shabby coats, stood before them, pallet and brushes in hand; and women by the score, — some of them young and pleasing, with duennas patiently waiting near by; but more often they were neither young nor beautiful, and with an evident renunciation of pomps and vanities. We glanced at their copies curiously. Sometimes they seemed the original in miniature, and sometimes, — ah well, we all fail.

We looked in upon the annual exhibition of pictures at the Palais de l'Industrie one day, and were particularly impressed with the *nudité* of the modern school of French art. Pink-tinted flesh may be very beautiful, but there must be something higher! We saw there, too, another day, the clock on exhibition for a time before being consigned to its destined place at Beauvais. It was even more wonderful than the one so famous at Strasbourg. This was of the size of an ordinary church organ, and of similar shape; a mass of gilt and chocolate-colored wood; a mass of dials, great and small — of time tables, and, indeed, of tables for computing everything earthly and heavenly, with dials to show the time in fifty different places, and everything else that could, by any possible connection with time, be supposed to belong to a clock. Upon the top, Christ, seated in an arm-chair, was represented as judging the world, his feet upon the clouds; on either side kneeling female figures adored him. Just below, a pair of scales bided their time. On every peak stood little images, while fifty puppets peeped out of fifty windows. Just below the image of the Saviour, a figure emerged through an open door at the striking of every quarter of an hour,—coming out with a slide and occasional jerk by no means graceful. **We** had an opportunity of observing all this in the three quarters of an hour of waiting. We viewed the clock upon every side, being especially interested in a picture at one point representing a rocky coast, a light-house, and a long stretch of waves upon which labored two ships attached in some way to the works within. They pitched back **and forth** without making any progress whatever, in a way very suggestive to us, who had lately suffered from a similar motion. **A** dozen **priests** seated themselves with us upon the bench before the clock as the hand approached the hour. They wore the long black robes and odd little skull-caps, that fit so like a plaster, and which are, I am sure, kept in place by some law of attraction unknown to us. One, of a different order, or higher grade, in a shorter robe and with very thin legs, encased in black stockings that added to their shadowy appearance, shuffled up to his place just in time to throw back his head and open his mouth as the clock struck, and the last judgment began. The cock upon the front gave a preliminary and weak flap of his wings, and emitted **three** feeble, squeaky crows, that must, I am sure, have **convulsed** the very puppets. Certainly they all disappeared from the windows, and something jumped into their places intended to represent flames, but which looked so much like reversed tin petticoats, that we supposed for a moment they were all standing on their **heads.** All the figures upon the peaks turned their backs upon us. The image of Christ began to wave its hands. The kneeling women swayed back and forth, clasping their own. Two angels raised to their lips long, gilt trumpets, as if to blow a blast; then dropped them; then raised them a second time, and even made a third abortive attempt. From one of the open doors Virtue was jerked out to be judged; Virtue in a red gown. The scales began to dance up and down. An angel appeared playing a guitar, and Virtue went triumphantly off to the right, to slow and appropriate music, an invisible organ playing meanwhile. Then Vice appeared. I confess he excited my instant and profound pity. Such a poor, naked, wretched-looking object as he was! with his hands to his face, as though he were heartly ashamed to come out in such a plight. I venture to say, if he had been decked out like Virtue, he might have stolen off to the right, and nobody been the wiser. Good clothes do a great deal in Paris. As it was, the scales danced up and down a moment, and then the devil appeared with a sharp stick, and drove him around the corner to the left, with very distant and feeble thunder for an accompaniment. That ended the show. All the little puppets jumped back into all the little windows, and we came away.

Speaking of picture galleries, we spent a pleasant hour in the gallery of the Luxembourg — a collection of paintings made up from the works of living artists, and of those who have been less than a year deceased. It is sufficiently small to be enjoyable. There is something positively oppressive in the vastness of many of these galleries. You feel utterly unequal to them; as though the finite were about to attempt the comprehension of the infinite. One picture here, by Ary Scheffer, was exhibited in America, a few years since. It is the head and bust of a dead youth in armor— a youth with a girlish face. There are others by Henri Scheffer, Paulin Guerin, and a host more I will not name. One, a scene in the Conciergerie, "Reading the List of the Condemned to the Prisoners," by Müller, haunted me long after the doors had swung together behind us. The palace of the Luxembourg, small, remarkable for the beauty of its architecture and charming garden, built for that graceless regent, Marie de Medici, is now the residence of the president of the Senate; and indeed the Senate itself meets here. We were shown through the rooms open to the public, the private apartments of Marie de Medici among them, in one of which was a bust of the regent. The garden, like all gardens, is filled with trees and shrubs, flowers and fountains, but yet with a certain charm of its own. The festooning of vines from point to point was a novelty to us, as was the design of one of the fountains. Approaching it from the rear, we thought it a tomb,—perhaps the tomb of Marshal Ney, we said, whose statue we were seeking. It proved to be an artificial grotto, and within it, sprinkled with the spray of the fountain, embowered in a mass of glistening, green ivy, reclined a pair of pretty, marble lovers; peering in upon them from above, scowled a dreadful ogre—a horrible giant. The whole effect, coming upon it unexpectedly, was startling.

We had a tiresome search for this same statue of

Marshal Ney. We chased every marble nymph in the garden, and walked and walked, over burning pebbles and under a scorching sun, until we almost wished he had **never been shot.** At last, away **beyond** the garden, out upon a long avenue, longer and hotter if possible than the garden paths, we found it, — erected upon the very spot where he was executed. He stands with arm outstretched, and mouth opened wide, as though he were yawning with the wearisomeness of it all. It is a pity that he should give way to his feelings so soon, since he must stand there for hundreds of years to come. The guide-books say he is represented in the act of encouraging his men. They must have been easily encouraged.

Of the out-door gay life by gas-light, we saw less than we had hoped to see in the French capital. The season was unusually cold and wet, and most of the time it would have required the spirit of a martyr to sip coffee upon the sidewalk. One garden concert we did attend, and found it very bright and fairy-like, and all the other adjectives used in this connection. We sat wrapped in shawls, our feet upon the rounds of the chair before us, and shivered a little, and enjoyed a great deal. We went one night — in most orthodox company — to the Cirque de l'Impératrice, a royal amphitheatre with handsome horses, pretty equestriennes, and a child balanced and tossed about on horseback, showing a frightened, painful smile, which made of the man who held her a Herod in our eyes. A girl very rich in paint and powder, but somewhat destitute in other particulars, skipped and danced upon a slack rope in a most joyous and airy manner. When we came out, a haggard woman, with an old, worn face, was crouching in a little weary heap by the door that led into the stables, wrapped in an old cloak; and that was our dancing girl!

We went to the opera, too; it was Les Huguenots. To this day I cannot tell who were the singers. I never knew, or thought, or cared. And the bare shoulders flashing with jewels in the boxes around us, the *claqueurs* in the centre, hired to applaud, clapping their hands with the regularity of clock-work, the empty imperial box, were nothing to the sight of Paris portrayed within itself. You know the familiar opera; do think how strange it was to see it in Paris; to look upon the stage and behold the Seine and the towers of Notre Dame; the excited populace rising up to slay and to be slain, with all the while this same fickle French people serenely smiling, and chatting, and looking upon it — the people who were even then ready at a word to reënact the same scenes for a different cause. Just outside, only a day or two before, something of the same spirit, portrayed here for our amusement, had broken out again in the election riots. And we remembered that, as we drove around the corner to the opera house, mounted soldiers stood upon either side, while every other man upon the street was the eye, and ear, and arm of the emperor, who knew that the very ground beneath his fair, white city tottered and reeled.

We saw the emperor and empress one day, after having looked for them long and in vain upon the Champs Elysées, and in the Bois de Boulogne where gay Paris disports itself. It was the morning after the riot, when they drove unattended, you will remember, through the streets where the rioters had gathered. We were in one of the shops upon the Rue de Rivoli. Just across the way rose the Tuileries from the sidewalk. A crowd began to collect about the open archway through the palace, which affords entrance and egress to the great square around which the palace is built. "What is •it?" we asked of the voluble Frenchman who was gradually persuading us that brass was gold. "L'Empereur," he replied; which sent us to the sidewalk, and put from our minds all thoughts of oxidized silver and copper-colored gold. Just within the arch paced a lackey in livery of scarlet and gold, wearing a powdered wig and general air of importance. On either side, the sentries froze into position. The *gendarmes* shouted and gesticulated, clearing the streets. A mounted attendant emerged from the archway; there followed four bay horses attached to a plain, dark, open carriage; upon the front seat were two gentlemen, upon the back, a gentleman with a lady by his side. His hair was iron gray, almost silvery. He turned his face from us as he raised his hat gravely to the crowd, displaying a very perceptible bald spot upon the back of his head as he was whizzed around the corner and down the street. And that was Napoleon III. We saw no American lady in Paris dressed so simply as the empress. Something of black lace draped her shoulders; a white straw bonnet, trimmed with black, with a few pink roses resting upon her hair, crowned her head. She bowed low to the right and left, with a peculiar, graceful motion, and a smile upon the face a little worn and pale, a little faded, — but yet the face we all know so well. Beautiful Spanish woman, whose face was your fortune, though you smiled that day upon the people, your cheeks were pale, your eyes were full of tears.

There is nothing more wonderful in Paris than the tomb prepared to receive the remains of the first Napoleon, in the chapel of the Hôtel des Invalides; fitting, it would seem to be, that he should rest here among his old soldiers. We left the carriage at the gateway, and crossed the open court, mounted the wide steps, followed the half dozen other parties through the open doors, and this was what we saw. At the farther end of the great chapel or church, an altar, approached by wide, marble steps; gilt and candles embellished it, and a large, gilt cross upon it bore an image of the crucified Lord. All this was not unlike what we had seen many times. But four immense twisted columns rose from its four corners — columns of Egyptian marble, writhing like spotted serpents. They supported a canopy of gold, and the play of lights upon this, through the stained windows above and on either side, was indescribable. As we entered the door, darkness enveloped it, save where an invisible sun seemed to touch the roof of gold and rest lightly upon the pillars; an invisible sun, indeed, for, without, the sky was heavy with clouds. As we advanced, this unearthly light touched new points — the gilded candlesticks, the dying Saviour, but above all the writhings of these monster serpents, until the whole seemed a thing of life, a something which grew and expanded every moment, and was almost fearful to look upon. Filling the **centre of the chapel was a** circular marble wall breast-high. Do you remember, in going to the old Senate chamber **at**

Washington, after passing through the rotunda, the great marble well-curb down which you could look into the room below? This was like that, only more vast. Over it leaned a hundred people, at least, gazing down upon what? A circular, roofless room, a crypt to hold a tomb; each pillar around its circumference was the colossal figure of a woman; between these hung the tattered tri-colors borne in many a fierce conflict, beneath the burning suns of Egypt and over the dreary snows of Russia, with seventy colors captured from the enemies of France. A wreath of laurel in the mosaic floor surrounded the names Austerlitz, Marengo, Friedland, Jena, Wagram, Moscow, and Pyramids, and in the centre rose the sarcophagus of Finland granite, prepared to hold the body of him whose ambition knew no bounds. The letter N upon one polished side was the only inscription it bore. He who wrote his name in blood needed no epitaph. The entrance to this crypt is through bronze doors, behind the altar, and gained by passing under it. On either side stood a colossal figure in bronze; kings they seemed to be, giant kings, in long black robes and with crowns of black upon their heads. One held, upon the black cushion in his hands, a crown of gold and a golden sword; the other, a globe crowned with a cross and a golden sceptre. They were so grand, and dark, and still, they gazed upon us so fixedly from out their great, grave eyes, that I felt a chill in all my bones. They guard his tomb. They hold his sword and sceptre while he sleeps. I almost expected the great doors to swing open at the touch of his hand, and to see him come forth. Over these doors were his own words:

"I desire that my ashes may repose upon the banks of the Seine, in the midst of the French people I have loved so well." On either side, as we came out, we read upon the tombs the names of Bertrand and Duroc,— faithful in death! We wondered idly whose remains were guarded in the simple tomb near the door. It was surrounded by an iron railing, and bore no inscription. Who can it be, we said, that is nameless here among the brave? Little did we imagine at the time that here rested the body of the great Napoleon, as it was brought from St. Helena; but his spirit seemed to pervade the very atmosphere, and we came out into the gloom of the day as though we had, indeed, come from the presence of the dead.

CHAPTER VII.

SIGHTS IN THE BEAUTIFUL CITY.

The Gobelin tapestry. — How and where it is made. — Père la-Chaise. — Poor Rachel! — The baby establishment. — " Now I lay me." — The little mother. — The old woman who lived in a shoe. — The American chapel. — Beautiful women and children. — The last conference-meeting. — " I'm a proof-reader, I am."

BY no means least among the places of interest in Paris is the manufactory of the Gobelin tapestry which serves to adorn the walls of the palace *salons*. O, these long, tiresome *salons*, which must be visited, though your head is ready to burst with seeing, your feet to drop off with sliding and slipping over the polished floors. The wicked *stand* upon slippery places, and nothing so convinced us of the demoralizing effect of foreign travel as our growing ability to do the same. When you have seen one or two, you have seen all. There may be degrees in gorgeous splendor, but we were filled with all the appropriate and now-forgotten emotions at sight of the first, and one cannot be more than full. Many of the old palace apartments are dull and dingy beyond belief, by no means the marble halls of our dreams; but of the others let me say something once for all.

Under your feet is the treacherous, bare floor of dark wood, laid in diamonds, squares, &c.; over your head, exquisite frescoes of gods and goddesses, and all manner of unearthly and impossible beings enveloped in clouds by the bale,— usually an apotheosis of some king or queen, or both, and, as a rule, of the most wicked known at that time. The Medici were especially glorified and raised above the flesh,— and they had need to be. On every side pictures in Gobelin tapestry, framed into the walls, often so large as to cover the entire space from corner to corner, from cornice to within a few feet of the floor, and in this latter space doors, formed of a panel sometimes, for the entrance and egress of servants. Imagine, with all this, the gilt, and stucco, and wood-carving; the flowers, and arabesques, and entwined initials; the massive chandeliers, with glittering pendants; the mantels of rare marbles, of porphyry, and malachite; the cabinets, and tables, and escritoires of marqueterie and mosaic; the gilded chairs, stiff and stark, richly covered; the bronzes, vases, and curious clocks: and over all the air of having never been used from all time, and of continuing to be a bare show to all eternity,— and you have a faint conception of the *salons* of half the palaces.

As for the tapestry, pray don't confound it with the worsted dogs and Rebekahs-at-the-Well with which we sometimes adorn (?) our homes, since one would never in any way suggest the other. In these every delicate line is faithfully reproduced, and the effect exactly that of an oil painting. After long years the colors fade; and we were startled sometimes, in the old palaces, to come upon one of these gray shadows of pictures, out from which, perhaps, a pair of wonderful eyes alone would seem to shine. In old times the rough walls of the grim prison palaces were hung with tapestry wrought by the fair fingers of court ladies, the designs of tournament and battle being rudely sketched by gay gallants. Many a bright dream was worked into the canvas, I doubt not, never found upon the pattern; many a sweet word said over the task that beguiled the dull hours, and kept from mischief idle hands. But in the reign of Louis XIV. the art of weaving tapestry was brought from Flanders, and a manufactory established on the outskirts of Paris which still remains. To visit it a pass is required. Accordingly we addressed a note of solicitation to some high official, and in due time came a permit for Madame K. and family; and an ill-assorted family we must have appeared to the official at the gate. There were the rooms, hung with specimens of the tapestry, for which we did not care, and then the six devoted to the weaving; long, low, and narrow they were, with hand-looms ranged down one side. Through the threads of the warp we could see the weavers sitting behind their work, each with his box of worsteds and pattern beside him. The colors were wound upon quills, numbers of which hung, each by its thread, from the half-completed work. Taking one of these in one hand, the workman dexterously separated the threads of the warp with the other, and passed the quill through, pressing down the one stitch thus formed with its pointed end. You can imagine how slow this work must be. How tiresome a task it is to delight the eyes of princes! The making of carpets, which has been recently added, is equally tiresome. This, too, is hand work, they being woven in some way over a round stick, and then cut and trimmed with a pair of shears. To make one requires from five to ten years, and their cost is from six to twenty thousand dollars. About six hundred weavers are said to be here, though we saw but a small proportion of that number. They receive only from three to five hundred dollars a year, with a pension of about half as much if they are disabled.

From the Gobelins we drove across the Seine again, and out to Père la-Chaise, where stood once the house of the confessor of Louis XIV., from whom the cemetery takes its name, the Jesuit priest through whose influence the edict of Nantes was revoked. A kind of ghastly imitation of life it all seemed — the narrow houses on either side of the paved streets, that were not houses at all, hung with dead flowers and corpse-like wreaths, stained an unnatural hue. We peered through the bars of the locked gate opening into the Jews' quarter, trying to distinguish the tomb where lie the ashes of a life that blazed, and burned itself out. Poor Rachel! Through the solemn streets, among the quiet dwellings of the noiseless city, whence comes no sound of joy or grief, where they need no candle, neither light of the sun, we walked a while, then plucked a leaf or two, and came away.

One day, when the sun lay hot upon the white streets of the beautiful city, we searched among the shops of the crooked Faubourg St. Honoré for a number forgotten now, and the Crêche, where the working mothers may leave their children during the day. In another and more quiet street we found it. We pulled the bell before a massive gateway; the wide doors opened upon a smiling portress, who led the way across the paved court to the house, where she pointed up some stairs, and left us to mount and turn until it was no longer possible, until a confusion of doors barred our way, when we rapped upon one. Another was opened, and we found ourselves among the babies. There were, perhaps, twenty in all, the larger children being in the school-room below; but even twenty toddling, rolling babies, looking so very like the same image done in putty over and over again, appears an alarming and unlimited number when taken in a body. They rolled beneath our feet, they clung to our skirts, they peeped out, finger in mouth, from behind the doors, they kicked pink toes up from the swinging cradles, and in fact, like the clansmen of Rhoderic Dhu, appeared in a most startling manner from the most unexpected places. Plump little things they were, encased in shells of blue-checked aprons, from the outer one of which they were surreptitiously slipped upon our entrance to disclose a fresher one beneath. How long this process could have continued with a similar happy result, we did not inquire. Every head was tied up in a tight little night-cap, giving them the appearance of so many little bag puddings. Every face was a marvel of health and contentment, with one kicking, screaming exception upon the floor. "Eengleesh," explained the Sister of Charity who seemed to have them in charge, giving a sweeping wipe to the eyes, nose, and mouth, gradually liquidizing, of this one, and trying in vain to pacify a nature that seemed peaceless. Who was its mother, or how the little stranger chanced to be here, we did not learn. On either side of the long, narrow room hung the white-curtained cradles, each with its pretty, pink quilt. At one end was an altar, most modest in its appointments, consisting of hardly more than a crucifix and a vase of flowers upon the mantel. As we entered the room, the sister stood before it with a circle of white caps and blue checked aprons around her, a circle of little clasped hands, of upturned eyes and lisping lips, repeating what might have been, "Now I lay me," for anything we knew. Our entrance brought wandering eyes and thoughts.

At the opposite end of the room, a wide, long window swung open, revealing a pleasant garden down below, all green and blossoming, with an image of the Virgin half hid among the vines. Cool, and fresh, and green it seemed after the glare of the hot streets, a pleasant picture for the baby eyes. Out from this window the little feet could trot upon the guarded roof of a piazza. A little chair, a broken doll, and limbless horse here were familiar objects to the eyes of the mothers in our party, and when two children seized upon one block with a determination which threatened a breach of the peace, we were convinced that even baby nature was the same the world over. Supper time came, and the children were gathered together in a small room, before the drollest little table imaginable — a kind of elongated doughnut, raised a foot from the floor, with a circular seat around it. All the little outer shells of blue check were slipped on, all the little fat bodies lifted over and set into their places, to roll off, or about, at will. A grace was said, to us, I think, since all the little eyes turned towards us, and a plate of oatmeal porridge put before each one. Some ate with a relish, and a painful search over the face with a spoon for the open, waiting mouth; some leaned back to stare at the company; and others persisted in dipping into the dish of their next neighbor. One little thing, hardly more than a year old, drew down the corners of her mouth in a portentous manner, when the motherly one beside her, of the advanced age of three years, perhaps, rapped on the table with her spoon, and patted the doleful little face, smiling all the while, until she actually drew out smiles in return. The dear little mother! An attendant with a homely face, creased into all manner of good-natured lines, resolved herself into the old woman who lived in a shoe, holding two babies and the porridge dish in her lap, balancing one upon the end of the low bench beside her, while two or three more stood at her knee, clinging to her apron. It was like a nest of open-mouthed birdlings. Blessings on the babies, and those, whether of our faith or not, who teach and care for them, we thought, as we came away. "Inasmuch as ye have done it unto one of the least of these, ye did it unto me," said the Master.

Although I said nothing of our church-going in London, I cannot pass over our American chapel in Paris, with its carved, umbrella-like canopy, shading the good Dr. R., who did so much socially, as well as spiritually, for Americans there. Here came many whose names are well known; among them our minister to France, an elderly gentleman of unpretending dress and manner, with a kindly, care-worn face. And here gathered also a company of beautiful women and children, proving the truth of all that has been said of our countrywomen. A blending of all types were they, as our people are a blending of all nationalities, each more lovely than the other, and all making up a picture well worth seeing. I wish I might say as much for the opposite sex. One gentleman, who wore a red rose always in his button-hole, and turned his back upon the minister to stare at the women, had a handsome though *blasé* face, and more than one head above the pews would have been marked anywhere; but the women and children bore away the palm. The delicate, sensitive faces which characterize American women, whether the effect of climate, manner of life, or of the nerves for which we are so celebrated, are found nowhere else, I am sure.

Besides the Sabbath services a weekly prayer-meeting was held here. They were singing some sweet familiar hymn as we entered one evening and took our place among the pilgrims and strangers like ourselves. It was the last gathering for the winter. Some were off for home, some for a summer of travel; only a few, with the pastor, were to remain. One followed another in words of retrospection, and regret at parting, until a pall settled over the little company — until even we, who had never been there before, wiped our eyes because of the general dolefulness. A hush and universal mistiness pervaded the air of the dimly-lighted house; the assembly seemed about to pass out of existence, Niobe-like. Then up rose Dr. R., the pastor. I wondered what he could say to add to the gloom; something like this, perhaps: "Dear people, everybody is off; let us shut up the church, lock the door, and throw away the key. Receive the benediction." But no; I wish you might feel the thrill that went through the little company as his words fell from his lips. I wish I dared attempt to repeat them. "And now to you who go," he said, at last, "who take with you something of our hearts, be sure our prayers will follow you. Keep us in memory; but, above all, keep in memory your church vows. Make yourselves known as Christians among Christians. And when you have reached home — the home to which our thoughts have so often turned together — let this be a lesson. When summer comes and you leave the city for the country, for the mountains, for the sea-side, take your religion with you. Search out some struggling little church with a discouraged pastor, — you'll not look far or long to find such a one, — and work for that, as you have worked for us. And one thing more; send your friends who are coming abroad to us. Send us the Christians, for we need them, and by all means send us those who are not Christians; they may need us; and the Lord bless you, and keep you in all your goings, and give you peace."

Then the people gathered in knots for last words — for hand-clasps and good-byes. Now a spirit of peace and good will having fallen upon us with the pastor's benediction, we gazed wistfully upon the strangers in the hope of finding one familiar face; but there was none; so we came sorrowfully down the aisle. The door was almost reached when a sharp, twanging voice behind us began, "I'm sent out by X. & Y., book publishers." "O," said I to the friend at my side, "I believe I will speak to that man. I know Mr. X., and I do so want to speak to somebody." How he accomplished the introduction I cannot tell, but in a moment my hand was grasped by that of a stout little man, with bushy hair and twinkling eyes. "Know Mr. X.? Mr. Q. X.?" he began. To tell the truth I had not that honor, my acquaintance having been with his brother; but there was no time to explain, and retreat was equally impossible; so I replied that my father knew him well; then thinking that something more was necessary to explain the sudden and intense interest manifested in his behalf, added, desperately, "indeed, intimately." To this he paid no manner of attention, — I doubt if he heard it, — but rattled on : "Fine man, Mr. X., Mr. Q. X. Know Mr. Y.? Fine man, Mr. Y.; been abroad a year; I'm goin' out to meet him, I am. He's in Switzerland, Mr. Y. is; been abroad a year. I'm a proof-reader, I am. I s'pose you know what a proof-reader is." "Yes," I succeeded in inserting while he took breath, remembering some amateur attempts of my own in that direction. He began anew: "I'm sent out by X. & Y.; expect to find Mr. Y. in Switzerland; fine man —" Will he never stop, I thought, beginning a backward retreat from the pew down the aisle, with all the while ringing in my ears, "I'm a proof-reader, I am," &c. "Don't laugh, pray don't," I said to the friends waiting at the door. "It's dreadful — is it not?" What became of him we never knew, but in all probability the sexton removed him — still vocal — to the sidewalk that night; where, since we do not know for how long a time he was wound up, he may be iterating and reiterating to this day the interesting fact of his occupation, with the eulogy upon Messrs. X. & Y.

CHAPTER VIII.

SHOW PLACES IN THE SUBURBS OF PARIS.

The river omnibuses. — Sèvres and its porcelain. — St. Cloud as it was. — The crooked little town. — Versailles. — Eugenie's " spare bedroom." — The queen who played she was a farmer's wife. — Seven miles of paintings. — The portraits of the presidents.

THERE are four ways of going to St. Cloud, from Paris, says the guide-book; we chose the fifth, and took one of the little steamboats — the river omnibuses — that follow the course of the Seine, stopping at the piers along the city, which occur almost as often as the street crossings. Very insignificant little steamers they are, made up of puff, and snort, and smoke, a miniature deck, and a man with a big bell. Up the river we steamed through a mist that hid everything but the green banks, the pretty villas whose lawns drabbled their skirts in the river, and after a time the islands that seemed to have dropped cool, wet, and green into the middle of the stream. We plunged beneath the dark arches of the stone bridges — the Pont d'Alma not to be forgotten, with its colossal sentinels on either side of the middle arch, calm, white, and still, leaning upon their muskets, their feet almost dipping into the water, their great, stony eyes gazing away down the river. What is it they seem to see beyond the bend? What is it they watch and wait for, gun in hand? We pulled our wraps about us, found a sheltered place, and went on far beyond our destination, through the gray vapor that gathered sometimes into great, plashing drops to fall upon the deck, or, hovering in mid-air, wiped out the distance from the landscape as effectually as the sweep of a painter's brush, while it softened and spiritualized everything near, from the sharply outlined eaves, and gables, and narrow windows of the village struggling up from the water, to the shadowy span of the bridges that seemed to rest upon air. Then down with the rain and the current we swept again, to land at the forsaken pier of Sevres, from which we made our way over the pavings, so inviting in these French towns for missile or barricade, to the porcelain factory. No fear of missing it, since it is the one object of interest to strangers in the town; and whatever question we asked, the reply would have been the pointing of the finger in that one direction. Once there, we clattered and slipped over the tiled floor after a polite attendant, through its many show-rooms, and among its wilderness of pottery, ancient and modern. The manufactory was established by — I'm sure I don't know whom — in seventeen hundred and — something, at Vincennes, quite the other side of Paris; but a few years later, in the reign of Louis XV., was transferred to Sevres, and put under the direction of government. It is almost impossible to gain permission to visit the workshops, but a permit to pass through the show-rooms can easily be obtained. There were queer old-fashioned attempts at glazed ware here, some of them adorned with pictures like those we used to see in our grandmothers' china closets, of puffy little pink gentlemen and ladies ambling over a pink foreground; a pink mountain, of pyramidal form, rising from the wide-rimmed hat of the roseate gentlemen; a pink lake standing on end at the feet of the lady, and a little pink house, upon which they might both have sat comfortably, with a few clouds of jeweller's cotton completing the picture. A striking contrast were these to the marvels of frailty and grace of later times. The rooms were hung with paintings upon porcelain, the burial of Attila, which we had seen at the Louvre, among them. Every conceivable model of vase, pitcher, and jar was here — quaint, beautiful conceptions of form adorned by the hand of skilful artists, from mammoth vases, whirling upon stationary pedestals, to the most delicate cup that ever touched red lips.

At noon we strolled over to St. Cloud, a pleasant walk of a mile, beginning with a shaded avenue, rough as a country road; then on, down a street leading to the gates of the park of St. Cloud — a street so vain of its destination that it was actually lifted up above the gardens on either side. From the wide gates we passed into a labyrinth of shaded, clean-swept ways, and followed one to the avenue of the fountains, where we sat upon the edge of a stone basin to await the opening of the palace. For do not imagine, dear reader, that you can run in and out of palaces without ceremony and at all hours of the day. There is an appointed time; there is the gathering outside of the curious; there is the coming of a man with rattling, ringing keys; there is the throwing open of wide gates and massive doors, and then — and not until then — the entering in. As for the fountains, next to those at Versailles they have been widely celebrated; but as they only played upon Sundays and fête days, we did not see them. Their Sunday gowns of mist and flowing water were laid aside, and naked and bare enough **they were this day.** The wide basins, the lions and dolphins, were here, with the marble nymphs, and fauns and satyrs, that make a shower-bath spectacle of themselves upon gala days. When the hour refused to strike, and we grew hungry, — as one will among the rarest and most wonderful things, — we left the park, to find the crooked little town that sits in the dust always at the feet of palaces. Its narrow streets ran close up to the gates, and would have run in had **they** not been shut. Here in the low, smoke-stained room **of an inn** that **was** only a wine-shop, we spent the time of waiting, — our elbows upon the round, dark table, which, with the dirt and wooden chairs, made up its only furnishing, — sipping **the** sour wine, cutting slices from the long, melancholy stick of bread, all dust and ashes, and nibbling the **cheese** that might have vied with Samson for strength. The diamond-paned window was flung wide open, for the air seemed soiled and stained, like the floor. Just across the narrow, empty street, an **old** house elbowed our inn. The eaves of its thatched roof were tufted with moss, out from which rose a mass of delicate pink blossoms — pretty innocents, fairly blushing for shame of their surroundings. Through the long passage-way came the sound of high-pitched voices — of **a** strange jargon from the room opening upon the street, where a heavy-eyed maid, behind a pewter bar, served the blue-bloused workmen gathered about the little tables.

The white palace of St. Cloud, with its Corinthian columns, stood daintily back from its gates and the low-bred town; but its long wings had run down, like curious children, to peep out through the bars; so, you will see, it formed three sides of a square. It had lately been refurnished for the prince imperial. The grand *salons* need not be described; one is especially noted as having been the place where a baby was once baptized, who is now ex-emperor of France. In the same room the civil contract of marriage between **Napoleon I.** and **Marie Louise** was celebrated. A few elegant but less spacious rooms were interesting from having been the private apartments of the poor queens and empresses who have shared the throne of France. Gorgeous they were in tapestry and gilding, filled with a gaping crowd of visitors, and echoing to the voice of a voluble guide. Royal fingers may have touched the pretty trinkets lying about; royal forms reclined upon the soft couches; royal aching hearts beat to the tick of the curious gilt clock, that bore as many faces as a woman, some one wickedly said; but it was impossible to realize it, or to believe that high heels, and panniers, and jaunty hats upon sweet-faced, shrill-voiced **American girls** had not ruled and reigned here always, as they did this day.

Versailles lies out beyond St. Cloud, but we gave to it another day. We were a merry party, led by Dr. R., who left the train at the station, and filled the omnibus for the palace. There was an air of having seen better days about the city, which was at one time the second of importance in France; it fed and fattened upon the court, and when at last the court went away not to return, it came to grief. The most vivid recollection I have of the great court-yard, around which extend three sides of the palace, is of its round paving-stones — that seemed to have risen up preparatory to crying out — and the grove of weather-stained statues upon high pedestals, — generals, cardinals, and statesmen who hated and connived against each other in life, doomed now in stone to stare each other out of countenance. I am sure we detected a wry face here and there, to say nothing of clinched fists. It is a gloomy old court-yard at best. The front of the main building is all that remains of the old hunting-seat of Louis XIII., which his son would not suffer to be destroyed. It is of dingy, mildewed brick, that can never in any possible light appear palatial; and so blackened and purple-stained are the statues before it that they might have been just brought from the Morgue. The whole palace is only a show place now — a museum of painting and statuary. As for the celebrated gardens, we walked for hours, and still they stretched away on every side. We explored paths wide and narrow, crooked and straight, and saw clipped trees by the mile, with grottoes and the skeletons of the fountains that, like naughty children, play o' Sundays, and all the wonderful trees, shrubs, and **flowers** brought from the ends of the earth, and ate honey gingerbread (flavored with extract of turpentine) before an open booth, and were ready to faint with weariness; and when at last **a broad** avenue opened before us with the Trianons, which must be seen, at the farther end, we would not have taken the whole place as a gift. It must have been at this point that we fortified ourselves with the gingerbread.

The Grand Trianon alone were we permitted to enter. It is in the form of an Italian villa, with a ground floor only, and long windows opening upon delightful gardens. Like Versailles, it is now a mere show, although a suit of apartments was fitted up here some time since, in anticipation of a neighborly visit from Queen Victoria to Eugenie, making of the little palace a kind of guest chamber, a spare bedroom. As we followed a winding path through the park, we came suddenly upon an open glade, surrounded and shaded by forest trees. Over the tiny lake, in the centre, swans were sailing. Half hidden among the wide-spread, sweeping branches of the trees were the scattered farm-houses of a deserted village — only half a dozen in all, of rude, half Swiss architecture, made to imitate age and decay, quaintly picturesque. Here Marie Antoinette and her court played at poverty. Do you remember how, when she grew weary of solemn state, she came here with a few favored ones to forget her crown, and dream she was a farmer's wife? The dairy was empty, the marble slab bare upon which she made butter for her guests. Just beyond was the mill, but the wheel was still. It was a pleasant dream — a dream of Arcadia. Ah, but there was a fearful awakening! "The poorest peasant in the land," said the queen, "has one little spot which she can call her own; the Queen of France asks no more." So she shut the gates upon the people who had claimed and held the right, from all time, to wander at will through the gardens of their kings. Then they hated her, whom they had greeted with shouts of welcome when she came a bride from over the border. "The Austrian! the Austrian!" they hissed through the closed gates. And one day they dragged her out from a bare cell in the Conciergerie, — no make-believe of rough walls, of coarse fare there, — they bound the slender hands behind her, they thrust into a prison cart the form that had been used to rest upon down and silken cushions, and bore her over the rough stones to the scaffold. Ah, it makes one shudder!

To see the two hundred rooms of the palace of Versailles requires a day, at least; but we, fearful that this might be our last opportunity, determined to spend the remaining hour or two and our last atom of strength in the attempt. A wandering cabman pounced upon us as we came down the avenue from the Trianons, and bore us back to the palace, where we toiled up and down the grand stairway, and peeped into the chapel that had echoed to the mockery of worship in the time of the king who built all this — the king who loved everybody's wife but his own — so faithlessly! There was a dizzy hurrying through corridors lined with statuary, through one *salon* after another hung with Horace Vernet's paintings describing the glories of France — the crowning of its kings, the reception of its ambassadors, the signing of its treaties, the winning of its battles; but was all this bloodshed, and all this agony depicted upon canvas, for the glory of France? There were immense galleries, where, on every side, from cornice to floor, one was conscious of nothing but smoke and cannon, wounds and gore, and rolling eyes. We walked over the prescribed three miles and a half of floors slippery as ice, and gazed upon the seven miles of pictures, with a feeling less of pleasure or gratified curiosity than of satisfaction at having *done* Versailles. Room after room was devoted to portraits, full lengths and half lengths, side faces and full fronts; faces to be remembered, if one had not been in such mortal haste, and faces that would never have been missed from the ermined robes. In a quiet corner we were startled to find some of our good presidents staring down upon us from the wall. A mutual surprise it seemed to be. But if we Americans must be awkward and clownish to the last degree, half civilized, and but one remove from barbarism, don't let us put the acme of all this upon canvas, and hang it in the palace of kings. Here was President Grant represented in the saloon of a steamboat, — America to the last, — one leg crossed, one heel upon the opposite knee, and his head about to sink into his coat collar in an agony of terror at finding himself among quality. His attitude might have been considered graceful and dignified in a bar-room, or even in the saloon of a Mississippi steamer; but it utterly failed in both particulars in the Palace of Versailles, among courtly men and high-bred women.

CHAPTER IX.

A VISIT TO BRUSSELS.

To Brussels. — The old and new city. — The paradise and purgatory of dogs. — The Hôtel de Ville and Grand Place.— St. Gudule. — The picture galleries. — **Wiertz and** his odd paintings. — Brussels lace and an hour with the lace-makers. How the girls found Charlotte Brontë's school. — The scene of "Villette."

THERE were one or two more excursions from Paris, and then, when we had grasped the fat hand of Monsieur, our landlord, and kissed the dark cheeks of Madame, his wife, and submitted to the same from Mademoiselle, their daughter, with light hearts, serene consciences, and the —— family we started for Brussels. It is a six hours' ride by rail.

Almost as soon as the line between France and Belgium is passed, the low hills drop away, the thatch-roofed cottages give place to those of whitewashed brick, with bright, red-tiled roofs. All along the way were the straight poplars overrun with ivy, and the land was cared for, coaxed, and fairly driven to the highest point of cultivation. Women were at work in the fields, and more than one Maud Müller leaned upon her rake to gaze after us. Soon, when there were only level fields beneath a level sky, the windmills began to appear in the distance, slowly swinging the ghostly arms that became long, narrow sails as we neared them. At two o'clock we reached Brussels, after being nearly resolved into our original element — dust. Nothing but a sand-hill ever equalled the appearance we presented when we stepped from the train; nor did we need anything so much as to be thrown over a line and beaten like a carpet when we finally gained our hotel.

The old city of Brussels is crooked, and dull, and picturesque; but joined to it — like an old man with a gay young wife — is the beautiful Paris-like upper town, with its houses covered with white stucco, and a little mirror outside of every window, placed at an angle of forty-five degrees, so that Madame, sitting within, can see all that passes upon the street, herself unseen. Here in the new town are the palaces, the finest churches, the hotels, and Marie Therese's park, where young and old walk, and chat, and make eyes at each other summer evenings. Scores of strings, with a poodle at one extremity and a woman at the other, may here be seen, with little rugs laid upon the ground for the pink-eyed puff-balls to rest upon. Truly Brussels is the paradise and purgatory of dogs. Anywhere upon the streets you may see great, hungry-eyed animals dragging little carts pushed by women; and it is difficult to determine which is the most forlorn — the dog, the cart, or the woman. We never understood before what it was to "work like a dog." At one extremity of the park was the white, new Senate-house; opposite, the gray, barrack-like palace of the king; upon the third side, among others, our hotel. Here we were happy in finding another family of friends. With them we strolled down into the old town, after dinner, taking to the middle of the street, in continental fashion, as naturally as ducks to water; crossing back and forth to stare up at a church or into a shop window, — straggling along one after another in a way that would have been marked at home, but was evidently neither new nor strange here, where the native population attended to their own affairs with a zeal worthy of reward, and other parties of sight-seers were plying their vocation with a perseverance that would have won eminence in any other profession. Through crooked by-ways we wandered to the Grand Place of the old city — a paved square shut in by high Spanish-gabled houses ornamented with the designs of the various guilds. From the windows of one hung the red, yellow, and black Belgian flag. There was no rattle of carts, no clatter of hoofs. Down upon the dark paving-stones a crowd of women, old and young, with handkerchiefs crossed over their bosoms, were holding a flower-market. Just behind them rose the grim statues of the two counts, Egmont and Van Horn, — who lost their heads while striving to gain their cause against Spanish tyranny and the Spanish Inquisition, — and the old royal palace, blackened and battered by time and the hand of forgotten sculptors, until it seemed like the mummy of a palace, half eaten away. Just before them was the Hôtel de Ville, with its beautiful tower of gray stone, its roof a mass of dormer windows. It comes to me like a picture now — the gathering shadows of a summer night, the time-worn houses, lovely in decay, the tawdry flag, and the heads of the old women nodding over their flowers.

Brussels has a grand church dedicated to Saints Michael and Gudule. If I could only give to you, who have not seen them, some idea of the vastness and beauty of these cathedrals! But descriptions are tiresome, and dimensions nobody reads. If I could only tell you how far extending they are, both upon earth and towards heaven — how they seem not so much to have been built stone upon stone, as to have stood from the foundation of the world, solitary, alone, until, after long ages, some strolling town came to wonder, and worship, and sit at their feet in awe! We crept in through the narrow door that shut behind us with a dull echo. A chill like that of a tomb pervaded the air, though a summer sun beat down upon the stones outside. A forest of clustered columns rose all around us. Far above our heads was a gray sky, the groined arches where little birds flew about. Stained windows gleamed down the vast length, broken by the divisions and subdivisions, — one, far above the grand entrance, like the wheel of a chariot of fire. All along the walls, over the altar, and filling the chapel niches, were pictures of saints, and martyrs, and blessed virgins, that seemed in the dim distance like dots upon the wall. Muffled voices broke upon the stillness. Far up the nave a little company of worshippers knelt before the altar — workingmen who had thrown down mallet and chisel for a moment, to creep within the shadows of the sanctuary; market-women, a stray water-cress still clinging to the folds of their gowns; children dropping upon the rush kneeling-chairs, to mutter a prayer God grant they feel, with ever and anon, above the murmur of the prayer, above the drone of white-robed priests, the low, full chant from hidden singers, echoing through the arches and among the pillars, following us down the aisles to where we read upon the monuments the deeds of some old knight of heathen times, whose image has survived his dust — whose works have followed him.

After leaving the church we wandered among and through the picture galleries in the old palaces of the city,— galleries of modern Belgian art, with one exception, where were numberless flat old Flemish pictures, and dead Christs, livid, ghastly, horrible to look upon. The best of Flemish art is not in Brussels. Among the galleries of modern paintings, that of the odd artist, recently deceased, Wiertz, certainly deserves mention. It contains materials for a fortune to an enterprising Yankee. The subjects of the pictures are allegorical, parabolical, and diabolical, the scenes being laid in heaven, hell, and mid-air. In one, Napoleon I. is represented surrounded by the flames of hell, folding his arms in the Napoleonic attitude, while his soldiers crowd around him to hold up maimed limbs and ghastly wounds with a denunciatory and angry air. Widows and orphans thrust themselves before his face with anathematizing countenances. In fact, the situation is decidedly unpleasant for the hero, and one longs for a bucket of cold water. Many of the pictures were behind screens, and to be seen through peep-holes — one of them a ghastly thing, of coffins broken open and their risen occupants emerging in shrouds. Upon the walls around the room were painted half-open doors and windows with pretty girls peeping out; close down to the floor, a dog kennel, from which its savage occupant was ready to spring; just above him, from a latticed window, an old *concierge* leaned out to ask our business. Even in the pictures hanging upon the walls was something of this trickery. In one the foot and hand of a giant were painted out upon the frame, so that he seemed to be just stepping out from his place; and I am half inclined to think that many of the people walking about the room were originally framed upon the walls.

Brussels is always associated in one's mind with its laces. We visited one of the manufactories. A dozen or twenty women were busy in a sunny, cheerful room, working out the pretty leaves and flowers, with needle and thread, for the *point* lace, or twisting the bobbins among the innumerable pins in the cushion before them to follow the pattern for the *point appliqué*. When completed, you know, the delicate designs are sewed upon gossamer lace. Upon a long, crimson-covered table in the room above were spread out, in tempting array, the results of this tiresome labor — coiffures that would almost resign one to a bald spot, handkerchiefs insnaring as cobwebs, *barbes* that fairly pierced our hearts, and shawls for which there are no words. I confess that these soft, delicate things have for women a wonderful charm — that as we turned over and over in our hands the frail, yellow-white cobwebs, some of us more than half forgot the tenth commandment.

Table-d'hôte over, one evening, " Where shall we go? What can we do?" queried one of the four girls in our party, two of whom had but just now escaped from the thraldom of a French *pensionnat*.

"It would be so delightful if we could walk out for once by ourselves. If there were only something to see — somewhere to go."

"Girls!" exclaimed Axelle, suddenly, " was not the scene of *Villette* laid in Brussels? Is not Charlotte Brontë's boarding-school here? I am sure it is. Suppose we seek it out — we four girls alone."

"But how, and where?" and "Wouldn't that be fine?" chorused the others. There was a hasty search through guide-books; but alas! not a clew could we find, not a peg upon which to hang the suspicions that were almost certainties.

"I am sure it was here," persisted Axelle. "I wish we had a *Villette*."

"We could get one at an English library," suggested another.

"If there is any English library here," added a third, doubtfully.

Evidently that must be our first point of departure. We could ask for information there. Accordingly we planned our crusade, as girls do, — the elders smiling unbelief, as elders will, — and sallied out at last into the summer sunshine, very brave in our hopes, very glad in our unwonted liberty. A *commissionaire* gave us the address of the bookstore we sought as we were leaving the hotel. "There are no obstacles in the path of the determined," we said, stepping out upon the Rue Royale. Across the way was the grand park, a maze of winding avenues, shaded by lofty trees, with nymphs, and fauns, and satyrs hiding among the shrubbery, and with all the tortuous paths made into mosaic pavement by the shimmering sunlight. But to Axelle *Villette* was more real than that June day.

"Do you remember," she said, "how Lucy Snow reached the city alone and at night?—how a young English stranger conducted her across the park, she following in his footsteps through the darkness, and hearing only the tramp, tramp, before her, and the drip of the rain as it fell from the soaked leaves? This must be the park."

When we had passed beyond its limits, we espied a little square, only a kind of alcove in the street, in the centre of which was the statue of some military hero. Behind it a quadruple flight of broad stone steps led down into a lower and more quiet street. Facing us, as we looked down, was a white stuccoed house, with a glimpse of a garden at one side.

"See!" exclaimed Axelle, joyfully; "I believe this is the very place. Don't you remember when they had come out from the park, and Lucy's guide left her to find an inn near by, she ran,—being frightened,—and losing her way, came at last to a flight of steps like these, which she descended, and found, instead of the inn, the *pensionnat* of Madame Beck?" Only the superior discretion and worldly wisdom of the others prevented Axelle from following in Lucy Snow's footsteps, and settling the question of identity then and there. As it was, we went on to the library, a stuffy little place, with a withered old man for sole attendant, who, seated before a table in the back shop, was poring over an old book. We darted in, making a bewildering flutter of wings, and pecked him with a dozen questions at once, oddly inflected: *Was* the scene of

Villette laid in Brussels?" and "*Is* the school really here?" and "You *don't* say so!" though we had insisted upon it from the first, and he had just replied in the affirmative; lastly, "O, *do* tell us how we may find it."

"You must go so-and-so," he said at length, when we paused.

"Yes," we replied in chorus; "we have just come from there."

"And," he went on, "you will see the statue of General Beliard."

We nudged each other significantly.

"Go down the steps in the rear, and the house facing you —"

"We knew it. We felt it," we cried, triumphantly; and his directions ended there. We neither heeded nor interpreted the expression of expectation that stole over his face. We poured out only a stream of thanks which should have moistened the parched sands of his soul, and then hastened to retrace our steps. We found the statue again. We descended into the narrow, noiseless street, and stood, — an awe-struck group, — before the great square house, upon the door-plate of which we read, —

"PENSIONNAT DE DEMOISELLES.

HÉGER — PARENT."

"Now," said Axelle, when we had drawn in with a deep breath, the satisfaction and content which shone out again from our glad eyes, "we will ring the bell."

"You will not think of it," gasped the choir of startled girls.

"To be sure; what have we come for?" was her reply. "We will only ask permission to see the garden, and as the portress will doubtless speak nothing but French, some one of you, fresh from school, must act as mouthpiece." They stared at Axelle, at each other, and at the steps leading into the upper town, as though they meditated flight. "I cannot," and "*I* cannot," said each one of the shrinking group.

Axelle laid her hand upon the bell, and gave one long, strong pull. "Now," she said, quietly, "some one of you must speak. You are ladies: you will not run away."

And they accepted the situation.

We were shown into a small *salon*, where presently there entered to us a brisk, sharp-featured little French woman,—a teacher in the establishment,—who smiled a courteous welcome from out her black eyes as we apologized for the intrusion, and made known our wishes.

"We are a party of American girls," we said, "who, having learned to know and love Charlotte Brontë through her books, desire to see the garden of which she wrote in *Villette*."

"O, certainly, certainly," was the gracious response. "Americans often come to visit the school and the garden."

"Then this *is* the school where she was for so long a time?" we burst out simultaneously, forgetting our little prepared speeches.

"Yes, *mesdemoiselles;* I also was a pupil at that

time," was the reply. We viewed the dark little woman with sudden awe.

"But tell us," we said, crowding around her, "was she like — like — " We could think of no comparison that would do justice to the subject.

The reply was a shrug of the shoulders, and, "She was just a quiet little thing, in no way remarkable. I am sure," she added, "we did not think her a genius; and indeed, though I have read her books, I can see nothing in them to admire or praise so highly!"

"But they are *so* wonderful!" ventured one of our number, gushingly.

"They are very untrue," she replied, while something like a spark shot from the dark eyes.

O, shades of departed story-tellers, is it thus ye are to be judged?

"Madame Héger," she went on, "who still has charge of the school, is a most excellent lady, and not at all the person described as 'Madame Beck.'"

"And M. Paul Emmanuel, — Lucy Snow's teacher-lover," — we ventured to suggest with some timidity.

"Is Madame Héger's husband, and was at that time," she replied, with a little angry toss of the head. After this terrible revelation there was nothing more to be said.

She led the way through a narrow passage, and opening a door at the end, we stepped into the garden. We had passed the class-rooms on our right — where, "on the last row, in the quietest corner," Charlotte and Emily used to sit. We could almost see the pale faces, the shy figures bending over the desk in the gathering dusk.

The garden is less spacious than it was in Charlotte's time, new class-rooms having been added, which cut off something from its length. But the whole place was strangely familiar and pleasant to our eyes. Shut in by surrounding houses, more than one window overlooks its narrow space. Down its length upon one side extends the shaded walk, the "*allée défendue*," which Charlotte paced alone so many weary hours, when Emily had returned to England. Parallel to this is the row of giant pear trees,—huge, misshapen, gnarled,—that bore no fruit to us but associations vivid as memories. From behind these, in the summer twilight, the ghost of *Villette* was wont to steal, and buried at the foot of "Methuselah," the oldest, we knew poor Lucy's love-letters were hidden to-day. A seat here and there, a few scattered shrubs, evergreen, laurel, and yew, scant blossoms, paths damp, green-crusted — that was all. Not a cheerful place at its brightest; not a sunny spot associated in one's mind with summer and girlish voices. It was very still that day; the pupils were off for the long vacation, and yet how full the place was to us! The very leaves overhead, the stones in the walls around us, whispered a story, as we walked to and fro where little feet, that tired even then of life's rough way, had gone long years before.

"May we take one leaf—only one?" we asked, as we turned away.

"As many as you please;" and the little French woman grasped at the leaves growing thick and dark above her head. We plucked them with our own hands, tenderly, almost reverently; then, with many thanks, and our adieus, we came away.

"We have found it!" we exclaimed, when we had returned to the hotel and our friends. They only smiled their unbelief.

"Do you not know — can you not see — O, do you not feel?" we cried, displaying our glistening trophies, "that these could have grown nowhere but upon the pear trees in the old garden where Charlotte Brontë used to walk and dream?"

And our words carried conviction to their hearts.

CHAPTER X.

WATERLOO AND THROUGH BELGIUM.

To Waterloo. — Beggars and guides. — The Mound. — Chateau Hougomont. — Victor Hugo's " sunken road." — Antwerp. — A visit to the cathedral. — A drive about the city. — An excursion to Ghent. — The funeral services in the cathedral. — " Poisoned? Ah, poor man ! " — The watch-tower. — The Friday-market square. — The nunnery. — Longfellow's pilgrims to " the belfry of Bruges."

WE could not leave the city without driving out to the battle-field of Waterloo. It is about a dozen miles to The Mound, and you may take the public coach if you choose — it runs daily. Our party being large, we preferred to engage a carriage.

We left the house after breakfast, and passed through the wide, delightful avenues of the Forêt de Soignes, — the Bois de Boulogne of Brussels, — then across the peaceful country which seemed never to have known anything so disturbing as war. Beyond the park lies the village which gave its name to the battle-field, though the thickest of the fight was not there. In an old brick church, surmounted by a dome, lie intombed many minor heroes of the conflict. But heroes soon pall upon the taste, and nothing less than Wellington or Napoleon himself could have awakened a spark of interest in us by this time. Then, too, the vivid present blinded us to the past. The air was sweet with summer scents. Mowers were busy in the hayfields. A swarm of little barefooted beggars importuned us, turning dizzy somersaults until we could see only a maze of flying, dusty feet on either side. One troop, satisfied or despairing, gave way to another, and the guides were almost as annoying as the beggars. They walk for miles out of their villages to forestall each other, and meet the carriages that are sure to come from Brussels on pleasant days. They drive sharp bargains. As you near the centre of interest, competition is greater, and their demands proportionately less. We refused the extortionate overtures of two or three, and finally picked up a shrewd-faced young fellow in a blue blouse, who hung upon the step of the carriage, or ran beside it for the last mile or two of the distance. The village of Mont St. Jean follows that of Waterloo. It is only a scant collection of whitewashed farm buildings of brick. We rolled through it without stopping, and out again between the quiet, smiling fields, our minds utterly refusing to grasp the idea that they had swarmed once with an army; that in this little village we had just left — dull, half asleep in the sunshine — dreadful slaughter had held high carnival one July day, not many years before. Even when the guide, clinging to the door of the carriage, rattled over the story of the struggle in a *patois* all his own, hardly a shadow of the scene was presented to us.

As our horses slackened their pace, he stepped down from his perch to gather a nosegay of the flowers by the road-side, making no pause in his mechanical narrative — of how the Anglo-Belgian army were gathered upon this road and the fields back to the wood, on the last day of the fight; how many of the officers had been called at a moment's notice from the gayeties at Brussels, and more than one was found dead upon the field the next day, under the soaking rain, dressed as for a ball. He pushed back his visorless cap, uttering an exclamation over the heat, and adding, in the same breath, that just here, about Mont St. Jean, the battle waged fiercely in the afternoon, when Ney, with his brave cuirassiers, tried in vain to carry the position; and all the time, the summer sounds of twittering birds and hum of locusts were in our ears; the barefooted children still turned upon their axles beside the carriage wheels as we rolled along, and that other day seemed so far away, that we could neither bring it near nor realize it. One grim reminder of the past rose in the distance, and, as we drew near, swelled and grew before our eyes. It was the huge mound of earth raised two hundred feet, to commemorate the victory of the allies. Hills were cut down, the very face of nature changed for miles around, to rear this monument to pride and vain-glory. Upon its summit crouches the Belgian lion.

We turn from the paved road, when we have reached what seems to be a mass of unsightly ruins, with only a tumbling outbuilding left here and there. The whole is enclosed by a wall, which skirts also an orchard, neglected, grown to weeds. The carriage stops before the great gates. It is very cool and quiet in the shaded angle of the battered wall as we step down. It has been broken and chipped as if by pickaxes. Ah! the shot struck hardest here. The top of the low wall is irregular; the bricks have been knocked out; the dust has sifted down; the mosses have gathered, and a fringe of grass follows all its length. Even sweet wild flowers blossom where the muskets rested in **those** dreadful days. At intervals, half way up its height, a brick is missing. Accident? Ah, no; hastily constructed loopholes, through which the English fired at first, before the horrible time when they beat each other down with the butts of their guns while they fought hand to hand here, like wild beasts.

We enter the court-yard. Only a roughly plastered room or two remain, where the greed that gloats even over the field of blood offers *souvenirs* of the place importunately. In the centre of this court-yard may still be seen the well that was filled with corpses. It must have given out blood for many a day. Upon one side are the remains of the building used for a hospital in the beginning of the fight, but where the wounded and dying perished in torment, when the French succeeded in firing the chateau; for this is *Hougomont.*

We came out at the gateway where we had entered; crossed the slope under the shadow of the branches from the apple trees, and followed the road winding through wheat-fields to The Mound. Breast-high on either side rose the nodding crests; and among them wild flowers, purple, scarlet, and blue, fairly dazzled our eyes, as they waved with the golden grain in the sunshine. "O, smiling harvest-fields," we said, "you have been sown with heroes; you have been enriched with **blood!**"

It was a long, dizzy climb up the face of The Mound to the narrow foothold beside the platform where rests that grim, gigantic lion. Once there, we held to every possible support in the hurricane of wind that seized us, while the guide gave a name to each historic farm and village spread out before our eyes. Only a couple of miles cover all the battle-field — the smallest where grand armies ever met; but the slaughter was the more terrible.

Connected with an inn at the foot of The Mound is a museum of curiosities. Here are queer old helmets worn by the cuirassiers, hacked and rust-stained; broken swords, and old-fashioned muskets; buttons, and bullets even — everything that could be garnered after such a sowing of the earth.

In unquestioning faith we bought buttons stained with mildew, and bearing upon them, in raised letters, the number of a regiment. Alas! reason told us, later, that the buttons disposed of annually here would supply an ordinary army. And rumor added, that they are buried now in quantities, to be exhumed as often as the supply fails.

I remembered Victor Hugo to have said in *Les Misérables* something in regard to a sunken road here, which proved a pitfall to the French, and helped, in his judgment, to turn the fortunes of the day. But we had seen no sunken road. I mentioned it to the guide, who said that Victor Hugo spent a fortnight examining the ground before writing that description of the battle. "He lodged at our house," he added. "My father was his guide. What he wrote was all quite true. There is now no road such as he described;

that was all changed when the earth was scraped together to form The Mound."

We lunched at the inn, surrounded by mementos and trophies, and served by an elderly woman, whose father had been a sergeant in the Belgian army, then late in the afternoon drove back to town.

The pleasant days at Brussels soon slipped by, and then we were off to Antwerp — only an hour's ride. I will **tell you** nothing about the former wealth and commercial activity of the city — that in the sixteenth century it was the wealthiest city in Europe, &c., &c. For all these interesting particulars, see Murray's Handbook of Northern Germany. As soon as we had secured rooms at the hotel, dropped our satchels and umbrellas, we followed the chimes to the cathedral. The houses of the people have crept close to it, until many of them, old and gray, have fairly grown to it, **like** barnacles to a ship; or it seemed as though they had built their nests, like the rooks, under the moss-grown eaves. The interior of the cathedral was singularly grand and open. As we threw our shawls about us — a precaution **never** omitted — an old man shuffled out from a dark corner to show the church, take our *francs*, and pull aside the curtains from before the principal pictures, if so dignified a name as curtain can be applied to the dusty, brown cambric that obstructed our vision. Rubens's finest pictures are here, and indeed the city abounds in all that is best of Flemish art, — most justly, since it was the birthplace of its **master.** Rubens in the flesh we had seen at the Louvre; the spiritual manifestation was reserved for Antwerp; and to recall the city is to recall a series **of** visions of **which one may not** speak lightly.

Across from the cathedral, upon a wide wooden bench in the market-place we sat a moment to consider our ways — the signal for the immediate swooping down upon us of guides and carriages, and the result of which was, our departure in a couple of dingy open vehicles to finish the city. We crawled about the town like a diminutive funeral procession, dismounting at the Church of St. Jacques to see the pictures, with which it is filled. In one of the chapels was a young American artist, copying Rubens's picture of "A Holy Family" — the one in which his two wives and others of his family enact the part of Mary, Martha, St. Jerome, &c. Behind the high altar is the tomb of Rubens, with an inscription of sufficient length to extinguish an ordinary man. There was a museum, too, in the city, rich in the works of Rubens and Vandyck, and the fine park in the new part of the town, as well as the massive docks built by the first Napoleon, were yet to be seen. The older members of the party were in the first carriage, and received any amount of valuable information, which was transmitted to us who followed in a succession of shouts sounding as much like "fire!" as anything else, with all manner of beckoning, and pointing, and wild throwing up of arms, that undoubtedly gave vent to their feelings, but brought only confusion and distraction to our minds. Not to be outdone, our driver began a series of utterly unintelligible explanations, the only part of which we understood in the least was, when pointing to the docks, he ejaculated, "Napoleon!" At that we nodded our heads frantically, which only encouraged him to go on. Pausing before a low, black house, exactly like all the others, he pointed to it with his whip. It said "Hydraulics" upon a rickety sign over the door. There were old casks, and anchors, and ropes, and rotting wood all around, for it was down upon the wharves. We tried to look enlightened, gratified even, and succeeded so well that he entered upon an elaborate dissertation in an unknown tongue. What do you suppose it was all about? Can it be that he was explaining the principles of hydraulics?

We made, one day, an excursion from Antwerp to Ghent and Bruges. We left the train at Ghent to walk up through the narrow streets, that have no sidewalks, to the cathedral. There was a funeral within. The driver of the hearse profusely decorated with inverted feather dusters, was comfortably smoking his pipe outside. A little hunchbacked guide, with great, glassy eyes, and teeth like yellow fangs, led us up the aisle to the screen beside the high altar, where we looked between the tombs and the monuments, upon the long procession of men circling around the coffin in the choir, each with a lighted candle in hand. As there were only about a dozen candles in all, and each must hold one while he passed the coffin, it was a piece of dexterity, at least, to manage them, which so engrossed our attention, that we caught but an occasional sentence from our guide's whispered story of the seventh bishop of Ghent, who donated the pulpit to the cathedral, and around whose marble feet we were trying to peep; of the ninth, who was poisoned as he went upon some mission ("Poisoned? Ah, poor man!" we ejaculated, absently, our eyes anxiously fixed upon one man to whom had been given no candle as yet); of the tall brass candlesticks, supposed to have been brought from England in the time of Cromwell, and a host more of fragmentary information, forgotten now. The whole interior of the church is rich in decoration, black and white marble predominating, with pictures of the early Flemish school filling every available space. Once out of the church, we climbed into an ark of a carriage, and drove about the city, our little guide standing beside the driver, back to the horses most of the time, to pour out a torrent of history and romance. A most edifying spectacle it would have been anywhere else. Do read Henry Taylor's "Philip von Artevelde" before going to Ghent: the mingled romance and history throw a charm about the place and people which bare history can never give. Veritable Yankees these old Flemish weavers seem to have been, with a touch of the Irish in their composition — always up in arms for their rights, and striking out wherever they saw a head. There is a new part to the city, with a grand opera-house, shaded promenades and palatial dwellings, but one cares only for the narrow, dingy streets, and the old market squares, in which every stone could tell a story.

We saw the tall, brick watch-tower, where still hangs the bell that tolled, —

"I am Roland, I am Roland! There is victory in the land,"

and the old Hotel de Ville, of conglomerate architecture, one side of which, in the loveliest flamboyant Gothic imaginable, seems crumbling away from its very richness. In the Friday-market square — it chancing to be Friday — was a score of bustling busybodies, swarming like bees. Here, in the old, quarrelsome times, battles were fought between the different guilds. I say battles, because at one time fifteen hundred were slain in this very square. Such a peaceful old square as it seemed to be the day of our visit! the old gray houses, that have echoed to the sound of strife, fairly smiling in the sunshine, and the market women kneeling upon the stones which have run with blood. At one corner rose a tower, and half way up its height may still be seen the iron rod, over which was hung imperfect linen, to shame the weaver who had dared to offer it in the market.

There is a great nunnery here in Ghent — a town of itself, surrounded by a moat and a wall, where are six hundred or more sisters, from families high and low, who tend the sick, weave lace, and mortify the flesh in black robes and white veils. When they become weary of it, they may return to the world, the flesh, and — their homes: no vows bind them. We drove along the streets past the cell-like houses where they dwell. Over the door of each was the name of her patron saint. It seemed a quiet retreat, a noiseless city, notwithstanding the six hundred women! But by far the most interesting sight, because the most ancient in the quaint old city, was the archway and turret of the old royal castle, erected a thousand years ago; only this gateway remains. Here John o' Gaunt was born. Built all round, and joined to it, are houses of more recent date, themselves old and tottering, and the arch beneath which kings and queens rode once, is now the entrance to a cotton factory.

We had only a few hours at Bruges — the city once

more powerful than Antwerp even, but where not a house has been raised for a hundred years, and where nearly a third of its inhabitants are paupers. But decay and dilapidation are strong elements of the picturesque, and nothing seen that day was more charming than a piece of wall, still standing, belonging to the old Charles V.'s palace — honey-combed, black, of florid Gothic architecture, rising from the quiet waters of the canal. At one end it threw an arch over the street, with a latticed window above it, beneath which we passed, after crossing the bridge. More than one picture of Bruges rests within my memory — its canals spanned by the picturesque bridges, and overhung with willows that dipped their long branches into the water, and the quaint old houses with many-stepped gables, rising sheer from the stream.

But with all its past grandeur, the old city is best known to us Americans through the chimes from its belfry tower, and we were some of Longfellow's pilgrims. We drove into the great paved Place under the shadow of the belfry tower when its shadows were growing long, and watched the stragglers across the square — women in queer black-hooded cloaks; chubby little blue-eyed maidens with school-books in hand; a party of tourists; and last, but by no means least, the ubiquitous American girl, with an immense bow on the back of her dress, and her eye fixed steadily upon the milliner's shop just visible around the corner. Almost three hundred feet the dingy brick tower rose above us, with low wings on either side, where were once the halls of some guilds, in the days when the tower was a lookout to warn of coming foes, — when the square was planned for defence. In a little court-yard, gained by passing under its arch, we watched and listened, until at last the sweet tinkle of the silver-toned bells broke the hush of waiting — so far away, so heavenly, we held our breath, lest we should lose the sound that fell

"Like the psalms from some old cloister when the nuns sing in the choir,
And the great bell tolled among them like the chanting of a friar."

We came back to Antwerp that night, tired, but triumphant, feeling as though we had read a page from an old book, or sung a strain from an old song.

CHAPTER XI.

A TRIP THROUGH HOLLAND.

Up the Meuse to Rotterdam. — Dutch sights and ways. — The pretty milk-carriers. — The tea-gardens. — Preparations for the Sabbath. — An English chapel. — "The Lord's barn." — From Rotterdam to the Hague. — The queen's "House in the Wood." — Pictures in private drawing-rooms. — The bazaar. — An evening in a Dutch tea-garden. — Amsterdam to a stranger. — The "sights." — The Jews' quarter. — The family whose home was upon the canals. — Out of the city. — The pilgrims.

AT nine o'clock, the next morning, we left Antwerp for Rotterdam. Two hours by rail brought us to a place with an unpronounceable name, ending in "djk," where we were to take a steamer. How delightful, after the dust and heat of the railway carriage, were the two hours that followed! The day was charming, the passengers numerous, but scattered about the clean, white deck, picturesquely, upon the little camp stools, drinking brandy and water as a preventive to what seemed impossible, eating fruit, reading, chatting, or pleased, like ourselves, with the panorama before their eyes. In and out of the intricate passages to the sea we steamed, the land and water all around us level as a floor; the only sign of life the slow-revolving arms of the windmills, near and far, with here and there a solitary mansion shut in by tall trees; or, as we wound in and out among the islands fringed with green rushes, and waving grasses that fairly came out into the water to meet us, and sailed up the Meuse, the odd Dutch villages that had turned their backs to the river, though their feet were still in the water over which hung rude wooden balconies, or still ruder bay-windows, filled with pots of flowers. This monotonous stretch of sea and land might grow tiresome after a while, but there was something peculiarly restful in that sail up the wide mouth of the river, beckoned on by the solemn arms of the windmills.

When we reached Rotterdam, how strange it was to find, instead of a row of houses across from our hotel, a wharf and a row of ships! Such a great, comfortable room as awaited us! with deep, wide arm-chairs, a heavy round table suggesting endless teas, and toast unlimited, and everything else after the same hearty, substantial manner. There was no paper upon the walls, but, in its place, paintings upon canvas. Delilah sat over the mantel, with the head of the sleeping Samson in her lap, and Rebekah and the thirsty camels were behind our bed curtains. From the wide windows we watched the loading and unloading of the ships, while the song of the sailors came in on the evening breeze, and with it, we half-fancied, the odor of sandal-wood and spices from the East Indiamen anchored across the way. Our hotel was upon the Boompjes, the quay that borders the river; but through nearly all the streets flow the canals, deep enough to float large ships. You can appreciate the advantage of sailing a ship to the very door of one's warehouse, as you might drive a cart up to unload; and you can imagine, perhaps, the peculiar appearance of the city, with its mingled masts and chimneys, its irregular, but by no means picturesque, houses, and the inhabitants equally at home upon water or land. Among the women of the lower classes may still be seen some national peculiarities in dress, shown principally in the startling ornaments — twisted gold wire horns, and balls, and rings of mammoth size thrust out from their caps just above their ears. Whether their bare red arms would come under the head of dress, might be questioned; but a national peculiarity they certainly were, and unlike anything ever seen before in the way of human flesh. Was that painfully deep magenta hue nature or art? We could never tell. There were some very pretty faces among the girls carrying milk about the city in bright brass cans, or in pails suspended from a yoke over their shoulders — faces of one type, round, red-cheeked, blue-eyed, with the mouth called rosebud by poets, and bewitching little brown noses of an upward tendency. As they all wore clean purple calico gowns, and had each a small white cap on their heads, the resemblance among them was rather striking. These caps left the whole top of the head exposed to the sun. Only an iron-clad, fire-proof brain could endure it, I am sure.

Not a beggar did we see anywhere in Holland. The people seemed thoroughly industrious and thrifty. A gentleman connected with the civil service there — an agreeable, cultivated man, who had been half over the world, written a book or two, and parted his hair in the middle — gave the people credit for all these, with many more good qualities, and added, "They are the simplest minded people in the world. Why, would you believe it, one of the canal bridges was run into and broken down, the other day, — a fortnight ago, — and it has been town talk ever since. No two men meet upon the street without, 'Have you heard about the bridge?'" And sure enough, when we reached the scene of the accident, in our after-dinner walk through the city, quite a crowd was collected to watch the passage of a temporary ferry-boat, the simplest contrivance imaginable, only an old barge pulled back and forth by ropes. Still later we found the entrance to a narrow street choked with people, though nothing more unusual seemed to be taking place than the bringing out of a table and a few chairs.

Upon the outskirts of the city are pleasant tea-gardens, often attached to club-rooms, where concerts are held Sunday evenings, attended by the upper classes. We walked through one, over the pebbled paths, and among the deserted tables, and then returned to see more of the town. It was Saturday night. All the little girls upon the street had their locks twisted up in papers so tight and fast that they could shut neither eyes nor mouth, but seemed to be in a continual state of wonderment. All their mothers were down upon their hands and knees, scrubbing the doorsteps and sidewalk, in preparation for the Sabbath. The streets were dirty and uninviting with a few exceptions, yet hardly more so than could be expected, when you remember that nearly the whole city is a line of wharves; but we felt no disposition to walk through it in our slippers, as the guide-book in praising its cleanliness, says **you** may. What an advantage it would be to the world if the compilers of guide-books would only visit the places they describe so graphically! We spent a quiet Sabbath here — the fourth of July — with not so much as a torpedo to disturb its serenity or mark the day, attending church at the English chapel, and joining in the responses led by a clear soprano voice behind us, which we had some desire to locate; but when we turned, at the conclusion of the service, there was only a row of horrible chignons to be seen, to none of which, I am sure, the voice belonged.

There is nothing to be seen in Rotterdam but its shipping. One great, bare church we did visit — "the Lord's barn;" **for** these cathedrals, stripped of altar, and image, and stained glass, and boarded into stiff **pews**, without the least regard to the eternal fitness of things, are ugly enough. There is somewhere here a collection of Ary Scheffer's works, — in the city I mean, — but we did not see it. It is less than an hour's ride by rail from Rotterdam to the Hague, with the same delightfully monotonous scenery all along the way — meadows smooth and green, and fields white for the harvest, separated by the almost invisible canals. No wonder the Spaniards held the Low Countries with a grasp of iron — the whole **land** is a garden. The Hague, being the residence of the court, is much after the pattern of all continental capitals, with wide, white streets, white stuccoed houses of regular and beautiful appearance, and fine, large parks and pleasure-grounds filled with deer, and shaded by grand old elms as large as those in our own land, but lacking the long, sweeping branches. A mile from the city is "The House in the Wood," the private residence of the queen of the Netherlands. The wood is heavy and of funereal air, but the little palace is quite charming within, though upon the exterior only a plain brick country-house. The rooms are small, and hung with rice-paper, or embroidered white satin, with which also much of the furniture is covered. The bare floors are of polished wood, with a square of carpet in the centre, the border of which was worked by hand. "Please step over it," said the neat little old woman who was showing us through, which we accordingly did. There was a home-like air, very unpalatial, about it all, — as though the lady of the house might have been entertaining callers, or having a dress-maker in the next room. Delicate trinkets were scattered about — pretty, rare things worth a fortune, with any amount of old Dutch china in the cosy dining-room. In one of the rooms hung the portrait of a handsome young man, — just as there hang portraits of handsome young men in our houses. This was the eldest son of the queen, — heir to the throne, — who, rumor says, is still engaged in that agricultural pursuit so fascinating to young men — the sowing of wild oats. In the next room was a portrait of Queen Sophie herself — a delicate, queenly face — a face of character. The walls of the ball-room are entirely covered with paintings upon wood by Rubens and his pupils. "Speak low, if you please," said our little old woman; "the queen is in the next room, and she has a bad headache to-day." I am sure she had a dress-maker! As we stooped to examine a rug worked by the royal fingers, an attendant passed, bearing upon a silver salver the remains of her majesty's lunch.

From the palace we drove back to town to visit two private collections of paintings. It seemed odd, if not impertinent, to walk through the drawing-rooms of strangers, criticise their pictures, and fee their servants. Upon the table, in one, were thrown down carelessly the bonnet and gloves of the lady of the house. I was tempted to carry them off. Only a vigorous early training, and the thought of a long line of pious ancestors, prevented. Here were pictures from most of the earlier and some of the later Dutch artists — Paul Potter's animals, Jan Steen's pots and pans, Vandervelde's quays and luggers, and green, foaming seas, and even a touch or two from the brush of the master of Dutch art. We stopped on our way back to the hotel, at a bazaar, — a place of beguilement, with long rooms full of everything beautiful in art, everything tempting to the eye, — and after dinner went out to one of the adjacent tea-gardens. It was filled with family parties drinking tea around little tables. The music was fine, though unexpected at times, as, for instance, when a trumpet blew a startling blast, and a little man in its range sprang from his seat as though blown out of his place. It was amusing and interesting to watch the stream of promenaders circling around the musicians' stand — broad, heavily-built men, long of body, short of limbs; women "square-rigged," of easy, good-natured countenance. I doubt if there was a nerve in the whole assembly.

At noon the next day, we took the train for Amsterdam — another two hours' ride. The land began to undulate as we went towards the sea, with the shifting hillocks of sand raised by wind and wave. We passed Leyden, famous for its resistance to the Spaniards, as well as for having been the birthplace of Rembrandt and a score of lesser lights, and Haarlem, known for its great organ, and still the sand-hills rose one above the other, until they shut out everything beyond. It was only when we made a sharp turn, and struck out in a straight line for the city, that the Zuyder Zee opened before us, the curving line of land along its edge alive with windmills. We counted a hundred and twenty in sight at one time, and still did not exhaust them; so many skipped and whirled about, and refused to be counted. It hardly seems possible that the city of Amsterdam is built upon piles driven into the sand and mud. Certainly, when you have been jolted and shaken until your teeth chatter, for a long mile, in one of the hotel omnibuses from the station through the narrow streets and over the rough pavements, you will think there must be a tolerably firm foundation. Such a peaceful, sleepy, free-from-danger air, these slimy canals give to the cities! You forget that just beyond the dikes the mighty, restless sea lurks, and watches day and night for a chance to rush in and claim its own. The canals run in a succession of curves, one within the other, all through the city. Upon the quays are the dwellings and warehouses. In the narrow streets, crossing them by means of endless bridges, are the shops and dwellings of the lower classes. Looking down a street, no two houses present an unbroken line. They have all settled in their places until they nod, and leer, and wink at each other, in a decidedly sociable, intoxicated manner. The whole city, to a stranger, is a curious sight — the arched bridges over the interminable canals; the clumsy boats (for the canals are too shallow to admit anything but coasters and river boats); the antic and antiquated houses with high gables, rising in steps, to the street; the women of the lower classes, with yokes over their shoulders, and long-eared white caps on their heads, surmounted by naked **straw** bonnets of obsolete fashion and coal-scuttle shape, and out and from which, on either side, protruded all the wonderful tinkling ornaments of which the prophet speaks; the long quays and streets utterly bare of trees; the iron rods thrust out from the houses half **way** up their height, upon which all manner of **garments**, freshly washed, hang over the street to dry. **Down in** an open Place stands the dark, square palace, grand and grim, where Hortense played **queen** a little time while Louis Bonaparte was king of Holland. Near the palace is a national monument, for the Dutch, too, remember their brave. There are old and new churches also to be seen, but churches bare of everything which clothes cathedrals with beauty, having been stripped in the time of the reformation. I suppose **one** should rejoice; but we did **miss** the high altar, the old carved saints, and the **pictures in** the chapels.

Some of the finest **paintings of** the Dutch school are in the national museum **here**; *genre* pictures, many, if not most of them, but pleasant to look at, if not of the highest art; and we visited another collection of the same, left by a M. Van der Hoop. There are several other private collections thrown open to the public.

But after all, the most charming picture was the Jews' quarter of the city. I know it was horribly filthy, and so crowded that we could hardly make our way; I know it was filled with squalor and rags, and great dark eyes, and breathed an odor by no means of sanctity. The dusky, luminous-eyed people seemed to move, and breathe, and hold a constant bazaar in the lane-like streets filled with everything known and unknown in merchandise, or leaning out from the windows of the tottering houses, their arms crossed over the sill, to dream away a lifetime. Still there was a fascination about it all, a suggestion of vagabondism, of Ishmaelitish wanderings, of having "here no continuing city," that touched the heart of a certain Methodist minister's daughter in our party.

Sometimes the houses rise directly from the water, as did our hotel, the entrance being gained from another street in front. Our room was like a town hall, with mediæval bed furniture and sofa, high chest of drawers, and great round table that might have come in with the Dutch when they took Holland. The deep windows looked down upon a canal. Across from them, anchored to the quay as if for a lifetime, was one of the river boats. Early in the morning the wife of the skipper — a square woman, brown-faced, with faded, braided hair — ran out bareheaded into the town, coming back with her arms mysteriously full. Down into the cabin she disappeared, from whence directly came a sound of sputtering and frying, with a most savory odor. Up she would come again — frying pan in hand to corroborate her statement — to call her husband to breakfast. He was never ready to respond, never, though he was doing nothing to support his energetic family at the time, but coiling and uncoiling old ropes, or rubbing at invisible spots with a handful of rope-yarn. I know he only delayed to add to his own dignity and the importance of his final advent. Breakfast over, there followed such a commotion in the little world as I cannot describe — a shaking out of garments, a scraping out of plates, and throwing into the canal the refuse of the feast, a flying up with pots and pans for no object whatever but to clatter down again with the same, and all in the face and eyes of the town, with nevertheless the most absorbed and unconscious air imaginable. When it was over, somewhat red in the face, but serene, the wife would appear upon the deck, to sit in the shadow of a sail and mend her husband's stockings, or put on a needed patch. We left the boat still fast to the quay; but I know that some day, when it was filled with scented oils, and rouge, and borax, and all the other things exported from the manufactories here, our skipper and his wife went sailing out of the canals and along the edge of the sea or up the Rhine, the stockings all mended, and the good woman not above giving a strong pull at the ropes.

To drive about the streets of Amsterdam is slow torture, so rough are the pavings, so springless the carriages; but to roll along the smooth, wide roads in the suburbs is delightful. Upon one side is a canal, stagnant, lifeless, with a green weed growing upon its still surface, which often for a long distance entirely hides the water; beyond the canal are pleasant little gardens and a row of low, comfortable-looking wooden houses with green doors. Before each door is a narrow bridge — a neatly-painted plank with hand-rails — thrown over the canal, to be swung around or raised like a drawbridge at night, making every man's house a moated castle. We passed a fine zoölogical garden here upon the outskirts of the city, a garden of animals that ranks next to the famous one in London; but had no time to visit it, nor did we see any of the charitable institutions in which Amsterdam excels.

"You know the pilgrim fathers?" said Emmie — whose family had preceded us by a day or two — the night after our arrival. "O, yes; had not our whole lives been straightened out after their maxims?" "Well, we've found the house where it is said they held meetings before they embarked for America. Wouldn't you like to see it?" Of course we would; in fact, it would be showing no more than proper respect to our forefathers. So six of us — women and girls — put ourselves under her guidance. We found a narrow, dirty street, the dwellers in which stared after us curiously. Between two old houses was an opening, hardly wide enough to be called an alley, hardly narrow enough to be looked upon as a gutter. Into this we crowded. "There; this is the house," said Emmie, laying her slight fingers upon the old stone wall before us. It was quite bare, and devoid of ornament or entrance, being evidently the back or side of a house. Down from the peak of the gable looked a solitary window. A rude balcony, holding a few plants, was below it, with freshly-washed clothes hanging from its rail. We rolled our eyes, experienced a shiver that may have been caused by awe or the damp chill of the spot, and came out to find the narrow street half filled with staring men and women crowding about the point of our disappearance, while from the upper end of the street, and even around the corner, others hastened to join the whispering, wondering crowd. How could we explain? It was utterly impossible; so we came quickly and quietly away; but whether this house had ever been a church, whether the pilgrim fathers ever saw it, or indeed whether there ever were any pilgrim fathers, are questions I cannot undertake to answer.

CHAPTER XII.

THE RHINE AND RHENISH PRUSSIA.

First glimpse of the Rhine. — Cologne and the Cathedral. — "Shosef in ter red coat." — St. Ursula and the eleven thousand virgins. — Up the Rhine to Bonn. — The German students. — Rolandseck. — A search for a resting-place. — Our Dutch friend and his Malays. — The story of Hildegund. — A quiet Sabbath. — Our Dutch friend's reply. — Coblentz. — The bridge of boats. — Ehrenbreitstein, over the river. — A scorching day upon the Rhine. — Romance under difficulties. — Mayence. — Frankfort. — Heidelberg. — The ruined castle. — Baden-Baden. — A glimpse at the gambling. — The new, and the old "Schloss." — The Black Forest. — Strasbourg. — The mountains.

WE had made a sweep through Belgium and Holland, intending to return by way of the Rhine and Switzerland. Accordingly, in leaving Amsterdam, we struck across the country to Arnhem, where we found a pleasant hotel near the station, outside of the town. Here we spent the night in order to break the monotony of the ride to Cologne. After climbing stairs to gain our room, wide, but so perpendicular that we were really afraid to descend by them, we had, from a rickety, upper piazza, our first glimpse of the Rhine, winding through flat, green meadows, with hardly more than a suggestion of hills in the distance. There is nothing of interest to detain one at Arnhem. The guide-book informed us that it was the scene of Sir Philip Sidney's death; but no one in the hotel seemed ever to have heard of that gentle knight — *sans peur et sans reproche.*

We reached Cologne at noon the next day. The road makes a *détour* through the plain, so that, for some time before gaining it, we could see the city nestling under the wings of the great cathedral. How can I tell you anything about it? If I say that it is five times the length of any church you know, and that the towers, when completed, are to be the same height as the length, will my words bring to you any conception of its size? If I say that it was partially built a couple of centuries before the discovery of America; that it was worked upon for three hundred years, and then suffered to remain untouched until recently; that the architect who planned it has been forgotten for centuries, so that the idea embodied in its form is like some beautiful old tradition, whose origin is unknown, — will this give you any idea of its age? The new part, seen from our hotel, was so white and beautiful, that, when we had passed around to the farther side, it was like waking from a sleep of a thousand years. The blackened, broken Gothic front told its own story of age and decay. Ah, the interminable dusky length of its interior, when we had crept within the doors! It was a very world in itself, full of voices, and echoes, and shadows of its own. We followed the guide over the rough stone floor, giving no heed to the tiresome details that fell in broken words and monotonous tones from his lips. I recall nothing now but the fact (!)

that behind the choir lie buried, in all their magnificence, the Three Wise Men of the East. As we came down one of the shadowy aisles, we paused before a fine, old, stained window. Our guide immediately became prolix again. "Dis," he said, pointing to one of the figures upon the glass, "is Shosef, in ter red coat; and dis is Shon ter Baptised; and dis, ter Holy Ghos' in ter form off a duff."

When the old woman at the door offered pictures of the cathedral, he assured us that they were quite correct, having been taken "from *nature, outzide* and *inzide*."

You must see the old Roman remains of towers and crumbling walls, sniff the vile odors of the streets, which have become proverbial, and be sprinkled with cologne — then your duty to the city is done. But almost everybody visits the Church of St. Ursula, which is lined with the skulls of that unfortunate young woman and her eleven thousand virgin followers.

The story is, that she was an English princess, who lived — nobody knows at what remote period of antiquity. For some reason equally obscure, she started with her lover and eleven thousand maidens to make a pilgrimage to Rome. Fancy this lover undertaking a continental tour with eleven thousand and one young women under his care! Even modern travel presents no analogy to the case. "And they staid over night at my aunt's," droned the sleepy guide, who was telling the story. The girls looked at each other. "Good gracious! what unbounded hospitality!" whispered one. "At his *aunt's!*" exclaimed a second, somewhat puzzled by the anachronism. "Don't interrupt," said a third interested listener; he means *Mayence;*" and he proceeded with the narrative. They accomplished their pilgrimage in safety; but, upon their return, were " fetched up py ter parparians," as the guide expressed it, which means, in English, that they were murdered, here at Cologne. If you doubt the story, behold the skulls! We turned suddenly upon the guide.

" Do *you* believe this ? "

" I mus; sinz I tells it to you," was his enigmatical reply, dropping his eyes.

The scenery along the Rhine from Cologne, for twenty miles, is uninteresting; just now, too, the weather was uncomfortably hot, and we were glad to leave the steamer for a few hours at Bonn. Upon the balcony of a hotel, looking out upon the river, we found a score of young men in bright-colored caps — students from the university here. When dinner was announced, they crowded in and filled the table, at which the ladies of our party were the only ones present. Such a noisy, loud-talking set as they were! When each one had dined, he coolly leaned back in his chair, and lighted his pipe! Before we had finished our almonds and raisins the room was quite beclouded. Then they adjourned with pipe and wine-glass to the balcony again, where we left them when we went out to see the town.

The university was formerly a palace, the guide-book had told us; but all our childish conceptions of palaces had been rudely destroyed before now, so that we were not surprised to find it without any especial beauty of architecture — only a pile of brown stone, three quarters of a mile long. I think we had left all the students drinking wine upon the balcony, for we saw none here, — though we went through the library, museum, and various halls, — except one party outside, who stared unblushingly at the girls remaining in the carriage.

Somewhere in the town we found a lovely old minster, through the aisles of which we wandered for a while, happy in having no guide and knowing nothing whatever about it. Outside, in a little park, was a statue of Beethoven, and in a quiet street near the water the musical girls of our party found the house where he was born. In the cool of the day we took another steamer, and went on towards the beckoning hills, at nightfall reaching Rolandseck. There was no town in sight, only a pier and three quiet hotels upon the bank, with a narrow road between their gardens and the water. We chose the one farthest away, and were rowed down to it, dabbling our hands in the water, and saying over and over again, "It is the *Rhine!*"

But the hotel was full; so we filled our arms with luggage, and walked back, up the dusty road to the second. A complacent waiter stood in the doorway, with nothing of that hungry, eager air about him which betokens an empty house; cool, comfortable-looking tourists, in enviable, fresh toilets, stared at us from the windows; a pretty German girl upon the balcony overhead was sketching the river and the Seven Mountains just below, uttering little womanly exclamations at times, ending in "*ach*" and "*ich*." After some delay, four single rooms were offered us; our party numbered twelve; we left a portion of our company here; the others went on — to the pier where we had landed, in fact, and with all meekness and humility sued for accommodations of the little hotel here, which we had at first looked upon with disdain. Fortunately, we were not refused.

When we came down the next morning, the sole occupant of the piazza opening upon the garden — where our breakfast was spread — was a stout, red-faced gentleman of general sleek appearance, who smiled a courteous "good morning." He proved to be a Dutchman from Rotterdam, who had in charge a couple of Malay youths sent to Holland to be educated — bright-faced boys, with straight, blue-black hair, olive complexions, and eyes like velvet. They were below us, walking in the garden now.

"We have but just come from Holland," we said, after some conversation; and, with a desire to be sociable, added that it was a very charming, garden-like *little* (!) country. (O dreadful American spirit!)

He smiled, showing his gums above his short teeth, and with a kind of enraged humility replied, —

"It is nothing."

"It is indeed wonderful," we went on, trying to improve upon our former attempt, and quoting a sentiment from the guide-book, "how your people have rescued the land from the clutch of the sea!"

But his only reply was the same smile, and the "Yes?" so fatal to sentiment.

"We visited your queen's 'House in the Wood,'" we ventured, presently. "Is it true that the domestic relations of the royal family are so unhappy?"

"O, the king and the queen are most happy," he replied. "You may always be sure that when *he* is in town *she* will be in the country."

This was a phase of domestic bliss so new to us that we were fain to consider it for a moment. Various other attempts we made at gaining information, with equally questionable success. Our Dutch acquaintance, though disposed to conversation, avoided the topic of his own country. Still he sought our society persistently, asking at dinner that his plate might be laid at the same table. Our vanity was considerably flattered, until he chanced to remark that he embraced every opportunity of conversing with English and American travellers, *it did so improve his English*. From that time we found him tiresome. Think of being used as an exercise-book!

It is here at Rolandseck that the romance of the Rhine, as well as its world-renowned scenery, commences. Across the river is the Drachenfels — the crag upon which the remains of a castle may still be seen, where, "in the most ancient time," dwelt Hildegund, a maiden beautiful as those of all stories, and beloved by Roland, a nephew of Charlemagne. When he went away to the wars, she waited and watched at home — as other maidens have done; but alas! instead of her lover, came after a time only the news of his death. Then Hildegund laid aside her gay attire and happy heart, with her hopes, and leaving her father's castle, came down to bury her young life in the nunnery upon the island at its foot. But the rumor was false; and in time Roland returned, only to find himself too late, for Hildegund was bound by vows which could not be broken. Then, upon the rock called now Rolandseck, the unhappy lover built a castle opposite the Drachenfels and overlooking the

Island of Nonnenworth. Here he could watch the nuns as they walked in the convent garden, and perhaps among them distinguish the form of Hildegund.

On our way down from the arch, which, with a few crumbling stones is all that remains now of Roland's castle, we passed through one of the vineyards for which the banks of this river are so noted. Do you imagine them to be picturesque? They are almost ugly. The vines are planted in regular order and pruned closely. They are not suffered to grow above three feet in height, and each one is fastened to a stout stake until the wood itself becomes self-supporting.

We spent a quiet Sabbath at Rolandseck. There was no church, no church service at either of the hotels. We rested and wrote letters, sitting in the grape arbors of the garden; only a low hedge and narrow, grass-grown road between us and the river. Down below, the rocks and the island shut out the world; across, the hills rose to the sky, their slopes covered with yellow grain, or dotted with red-roofed farm-houses, while tiny villages had curled up and gone to sleep at their feet. It was impossible to write. The breeze that rippled the yellow water blew away our paper and our thoughts; and when the steamer, puffing, and evidently breathless from stemming the current, touched at the little pier, we left everything and ran out to see the passengers disembark. A band played at the railroad station just above our hotel, and the park attached to it swarmed with excursionists during the afternoon. At dusk, when they had all gone, we wandered up the magnificent road which follows the course of the river; built originally by the

Romans, and said to extend for a long distance — five hundred miles or more — into Germany, returning with our hands full of wild flowers. When we went on board the steamer, Monday morning, we were closely followed by our Dutch friend and his Malays. They strolled off by themselves, as they seemed always to do; he joined our group under the awning spread over the deck. An English tourist seized upon him immediately, and when he had disclosed his nationality, proceeded with a glance towards us, to quiz him upon Dutch ways.

"Now, really," said the tourist, tilting back against the rail in his camp chair, "how dreadful it must be to live in a country where there are no mountains! nothing but a stretch of flat land, you know. I fancy it would be unendurable."

"Yes?" was the Dutchman's sole response.

"You still keep up your peculiar customs, I observe from Murray," the Englishman went on, loftily. "Your women carry the same old foot-stoves to church, I fancy. They hang up, you know, in every house."

"Ah!" and the Dutchman only smiled that same incomprehensible smile that had so puzzled us.

"And you smoke constantly," continued the inquisitor, growing dogmatic; "a pipe is seldom out of your mouths. Really, you are a nation of perpetual smokers."

"Yes," assented the Dutchman; "but then —" and here his eyes, and indeed his whole round, rosy face twinkled with irresistible humor, "*you know we have no mountains.*"

A shout went up from the listeners, and our English

acquaintance became at once intensely interested in the scenery.

The sail of half an hour to Coblentz was a continual delight. The rocky mountains rose abruptly from the water, terraced to their peaks with vineyards, or stood back to give place to modest towns and villages that dipped their skirts in the stream. At their wharves we touched for a moment, to make an exchange of passengers or baggage. Often from the lesser villages a boat shot out, the oars held by a brown-armed maiden, who boarded us to take, perhaps, a single box or bale, or, it might be, some bearded tourist with sketch-book under his arm. The passengers walked the deck, or gathered in groups to eat ices and drink the wines made from the grapes grown in these vineyards, with the pictured maps of the river spread out upon their laps, and the ubiquitous Murray in their hands.

As we neared Coblentz the villages increased as the hills vanished. Each had its point of interest, or monkish legend — the palace of a duke, a bit of crumbling Roman wall rising from the water — something to invest it with a charm. One — Neuwied — is noted for holding harmoniously within its limits, Jews, Moravians, Anabaptists, and Catholics. The Millennium will doubtless begin at Neuwied.

At Coblentz we remained a day, in order to visit the fortress of Ehrenbreitstein. From our windows at the hotel we could look directly across to this grim giant of rock, as well as down upon the bridge of boats which crosses the Rhine here. It was endless amusement to watch the approach of the steamers, when, as if impelled by invisible boatmen, a part of the bridge

"At the word of command they struck the most extraordinary attitudes."
Page 157.

would swing slowly round to make an opening, while the crowd of soldiers, market-women, and towns-people, waiting impatiently, furnished a constant and interesting study.

An hour or two after noon we too crossed the bridge in an open carriage, nearly overcome by the stifling heat, and after passing through the village of Ehrenbreitstein, ascended the winding road — a steep ascent, leading under great arches of solid masonry, through massive gateways, and shut in by the rock which forms the fortress. At various points, guards of Prussian soldiers, as immovable as the stone under their feet, were stationed. Suddenly in the gloomy silence, as we toiled slowly up, echoed a sharp tramp, tramp, and a line of soldiers filed by in grim silence, each one with a couple of loaves of bread slung by a cord over his shoulder. In a moment another line followed with a quantity of iron bedsteads, each borne solemnly upon the shoulders of four men. The guards accompanying them were armed, and wore queer, shining helmets. Still another company came swinging down to meet us, with fixed, imperturbable countenances, each bearing a towel in one hand, with military precision. They were on their way to the bathing-house upon the bridge.

Scattered about upon the broad esplanade at the summit, or rather arranged in lines upon the breezy, grass-grown space, were squads of recruits being drilled. At the word of command they struck the most extraordinary attitudes. Taking a tremendous stride, they endeavored to poise themselves on one foot, while they threw the other leg straight out behind into the air.

Being of all sizes, forms, and degrees of grace in movement, the effect, to say the least, was surprising; especially as the most intense silence and seriousness prevailed. A second stride and fling followed, then a third, when a pert young officer, of the bantam species, seized a gun, and strutting to the front, proceeded to illustrate the idea more **perfectly. At this** point our gravity gave way.

A young sergeant, with a stupid but good-natured face, attached himself to us in the capacity of guide. He could speak nothing but German, of which not one of us understood a word. We followed him from point to point, politely attending to all his elaborate explanations, and were surprised to find how many ideas we had finally **gained by** means of the patient and painful pantomimic accompaniment to his words.

The view from the summit is wonderfully extensive. All the kingdoms of the earth and the glory of them seemed spread **out** at our feet; and our fat little guide grew fairly red in the face in his efforts to make us comprehend the names of the various points of interest.

When we returned to the carriage the animated jumping-Jacks were still engaged in their remarkable evolutions; and as we came down we had a last glimpse of our Dutch friend and **his Malays,** who were making the ascent on foot.

The next day, though **passed** upon the beautiful river, was a day of torment. The stream narrowed; the frowning rocks closed in upon us, shutting out every breath **of air; the** sun beat down upon the **water and the** low awning over our heads with fiery **fury; in a moment of** idiocy we answered the call to *table d'hôte*, which was served upon deck with a refinement of imbecility just as the climax of the striking scenery approached. For one mortal hour we were wedged in at that table, peering between heads and under the awning which cut off every peak, making frantic attempts to turn in our places, as parties across the table exclaimed over the scenery behind us, and consoling ourselves with reading up the legends in the guide-book held open by the rim of our soup-plates, — of the Seven Sisters, for instance, who were turned into seven stones which stand in the stream to this day, because they refused to smile upon their lovers (fortunately for navigation, maidens in these days are less obdurate); of the bishop who shut his starving peasants into his barn and set fire to it, though his granaries were full, and who, in poetic justice, was afterwards devoured by rats; of the Lurlei siren, who lured men to destruction, and became historical from the individuality of the case; of various maidens bereft of lovers by cruel fathers, and of various lovers bereft of maidens by cruel fate, &c., while storied ruins crowned the crags on every hand, always half hidden under a weight of ivy, and often indistinguishable from the rock on which they seemed to have grown.

At Bingen, which is not especially "fair" from the river, the precipices drop away, the stream spreads out in nearly twice its former width, and is dotted with islands. At Mayence you may leave the steamer; the beauties of the Rhine are passed.

From Mayence we made an excursion to Wiesbaden; then on to Frankfort-on-the-Maine, to rest only a few hours, *doing* the city hastily and imperfectly; and finally reached Heidelberg at night, in time for *table d'hôte*. A talkative young Irishman sat beside us at the table, who spoke five or six languages "with different degrees of badness," he informed us; had travelled half the world over, but held in reserve the pleasure of visiting America.

"I have a friend there," he added, "though he is in *South* America."

"Ah?"

"Yes; at *Mobile*," he replied. "He held some office under government for a number of years, but during your recent war — for some reason which I do not understand — he seems to have lost it."

It did not seem so inexplicable to us.

Our conception of Heidelberg had been most imperfect. We knew simply that it held a university and a ruin. The former did not especially attract us, and we were sated with ruins. So, when we took possession of our lovely room, — a charming *salon*, converted temporarily into a bedroom, — it was with a kind of listless indifference that we stepped out upon the balcony before the window. And, behold! down below, an old, paved square, walled in by delightfully dingy old houses; a stone fountain; a string of waiting landaus (for Landau itself is near by), with scarlet linings to their tops — giving a bit of color to the picture; a party of German students crossing the square, wearing the caps of different colors to betoken different societies or clubs, and almost every one with a scarred cheek or suggestive patch upon his nose; and, lastly, on the right hand, and so precipitous as almost to overhang the square, a hill crowned with the castle, grand, though in ruins, which nature vainly tries to conceal.

There are ruins, and ruins. Except the Alhambra, in Spain, none in the world equal these.

What this castle must have been in the days of its glory, when it was the residence of a court, we could only faintly imagine. It is of red sandstone, and was a succession of palaces, built to enclose a square, or great court-yard, each of entirely different architecture and design, the *façade* of one being covered with statues, another having pointed gables, &c.; all having been erected at periods fifty or a hundred years remote from each other. At each corner were watch-towers to apprise of coming foes. You may still ascend the winding stairs of one, though the steps have been hollowed into bowls by dripping rain and mounting feet. Between these towers, upon one side, and on the verge of the hill, still remains the grand stone terrace,— where a hundred couples might promenade in solitude on moonlight evenings,— with summer-houses at each end; and beautiful gardens are still connected with the ruins. For all these palaces are in ruins. A few habitable rooms only remain among them all. Several sieges, and partial demolition at times, the castle suffered, and at last, a hundred years ago, lightning completed the work, since which time no efforts at restoration have been made.

The whole is overgrown with ivy, and embowered in shrubbery. Great trees spread their branches in the midst of the walls that still remain standing, and crumbling earth and drifting dust have filled many parts, even up to the broken window ledges of the second story. Across the broad stone steps leading to one of these palaces, tangled vines disputed right of way, and a neglected cherry-tree had scattered with wanton hand its over-ripe fruitage. Thrust through a casement was an ivy that might have vied with many of the trees around in the size of its trunk, and no artistic hand could have trailed its creepers with the grace Nature alone had displayed.

There was a grand banqueting-hall, with the blue heavens for a ceiling overhead. There was a drawing-room, the floor long since crumbled away, and only the broken walls remaining. Standing upon the loose earth, you may see the blackened fireplace far above your head, before which fair faces grew rosy centuries ago, and where white hands were outspread that have been dust and mould for ages. There was — But words cannot describe it, though I should speak of the winding ways like a labyrinth beneath it all; of the queer paved court-yard, from whence the knights sallied out in the olden time; of the great tower, split in twain by an explosion during the last siege; of the wine-cellars and the "Great Tun," upon which the servants of the castle danced when the vintage was gathered. In all attempts at word-painting there remains something that defies description, that will not be portrayed by language. And, alas! in that the charm lies.

We turned away from it with regret. One might linger here for days; but we had little time for dreaming.

The road from Heidelberg to Baden-Baden led through a charming country: indeed, we ceased to exclaim after a time over the cultivation of the land. So far as we saw it, the whole of Europe was a market-garden, with prize meadows interspersed. Not a foot of neglected or carelessly-tilled ground did we see anywhere.

We chanced to spend the Sabbath in this most un-Sabbath-like city of Baden-Baden. But so far as we knew to the contrary, it might have been a Puritan village. There was a little English chapel out in the fields beyond the city, where morning service was held, and our windows, overlooking a quiet square, told nothing of the gayeties of the town. It is an interesting old city in itself, built upon a side hill, full of unexpected stone steps leading from one street to another, and by and crooked ways, that were my especial delight. It being just now "the season," the town was full of visitors. The hot springs are of course the nominal attraction; the shops, parks, and new parts of the city, fine; but, after all, the interest centres at the Kursaal, or Conversation-haus. It is a great white structure, with a colonnade where it fronts an open square, and contains reading-rooms, *cafés*, a grand ball-room, and the gambling *salons*. Government has at length interfered, and these last, hired by companies paying a certain sum for the privilege of beguiling and beggaring visitors, were to be closed now in two years, I think, or less. In front of the Kursaal a band plays every afternoon; the colonnade and square are thronged with people promenading or occupying the chairs placed there, eating ices, drinking wine, and enjoying the fine music, but all perfectly quiet in manner and plain of dress. No one was gaudily or even strikingly attired. The Hanoverian women were the most marked for their queer head-dresses, consisting of an enormous bow and ends of wide, black ribbon perched upon their crowns, and giving their heads a peculiar, bat-like appearance. And in this connection I might say that national peculiarities in dress are seldom met with in the ordinary course of continental travel. They still exist to some extent among the lower classes, and are often assumed and perpetuated to attract the attention of travellers; but ordinarily you will find people whom you meet anywhere and everywhere to be costumed much alike. Paris fashions, with modifications (and in America with *intensifications*), have prevailed universally, until there are few outward dissimilarities to be observed among the people of different nationalities. Nothing strikes the attention of the traveller more than this universal homogeneousness; and not in dress alone. In Bruges, under the shadow of the belfry tower, little girls trot off to school in water-proofs, just as they do at home with us; and at the entrance to Stirling Castle, we passed a sturdy little boy with his hands in his pockets, whistling, "Not for Jo," exactly like other sturdy little boys we know at home.

But to return to Baden-Baden.

We almost fancied a sulphurous odor hung about the gambling *salons*. Not a footfall echoed upon the softly-carpeted floors as we entered. The most breathless silence hung over everything. In the centre, a crowd, three in depth at least, surrounded and hid the table covered with green cloth, before which sat the *croupier*, with a kind of little rake in his hand. In our eyes he was the incarnation of evil, though to unprejudiced vision he would appear simply a well-dressed — not flashily-arrayed — gentleman, of a rather intellectual countenance, who might have passed upon the street as a lawyer in good practice, or possibly a doctor somewhat overworked.

One after another of the bystanders covered the figures stamped upon the table with gold or silver. The ball in the centre, spinning in its circle, fell into a pocket with a "click." The *croupier* called the winning number I think (though confessing that the game is a hidden mystery). That quick, sharp utterance was the only sound breaking the silence. At the same time, with wonderful dexterity, he raked the money into a pile, and pushed it towards the winner, or, more frequently, added it to the pile before himself.

I looked in vain for any exhibition of excitement or anxiety among the players sitting or standing around the table. All were serious, silent; some few absorbed. Both sexes were equally represented, and old as well as young. Beside us was standing a woman with a worn, though still fine face, unobtrusive in dress and manner; a traveller and spectator, I judged, like ourselves. It was something of a surprise, not to say a shock, to see her suddenly stretch out her hand, and lay down a handful of gold pieces, selecting the numbers with an air that proved her to be no novice. "Click," fell the ball. The *croupier*, with a sweep of the rake, gathered up her Napoleons. The bank had won. Again she laid down her gold, placing each piece with thoughtful deliberation. Again they were swept away; and even the third time. She made no exclamation. She did not so much as raise her eyes from the table as she prepared to make a fourth attempt. There was no change in her face, except a certain fixedness which came over it, and a faint tinge of color rising in her cheeks.

We breathed more freely when we had gained the open air. I am sure there was an odor of sulphur about the place.

The scenery around Baden-Baden is striking and wild. Gloomy valleys abound, and dark forests cover many of the hills. We took a kind of wagonet one morning, and climbed the mountain behind the city, passing what is known as the "New Schloss," or castle, before leaving its limits. It is anything but *new*, however, having been erected some four or five hundred years. Its horrible dungeons, where all manner of torments were inflicted, and tortures suffered by the unfortunate wretches incarcerated here, attract scores of visitors. We went on, by the zigzag road up the mountain, to the Old Schloss upon its summit. This was the residence of the reigning family of Baden before the erection of the New Schloss. Hardly anything remains of it now but the walls of a square tower, from the battlements of which, by mounting to an encircling gallery, you may obtain a view well worth the effort. As far as the eye can see in one direction, extends the Black Forest — the very name of which brings to mind elfish legends innumerable. But; though our way led along its edge, so that we were shut in by the chill and gloom of the evergreens which give it its name, we saw neither elves nor gnomes, nor the traditional "wood-cutter, named Hans, who lived upon the borders of the Black Forest," about whom we used to read when we were children.

From Baden-Baden we took the railroad, following

the course of the Rhine to Strasbourg, spending only a night here, in order to visit the beautiful cathedral; then on to Lucerne, waiting an hour or two to break the long day's ride, at Basle. Here· the mountains began to grow before our eyes. We shot through tunnel after tunnel, cut in the solid rock, and suddenly sweeping around a curve, the everlasting hills wrapped in perpetual snows, greeted our astonished sight. We had reached the Mecca of our hopes at last.

CHAPTER XIII.

DAYS IN SWITZERLAND.

The Lake of Lucerne. — Days of rest in the city. — An excursion up the Righi. — The crowd at the summit. — Dinner at midnight. — Rising before "the early worm." — The "sunrise" according to Murray. — Animated scarecrows. — Off for a tour through Switzerland. — The lake for the last time. — Grütlii. — William Tell's chapel. — Fluellen. — Altorf. — Swiss haymakers. — An hour at Amsteg. — The rocks close in. — The Devil's Bridge. — The dangerous road. — "A carriage has gone over the precipice!" — Andermatt. — Desolate rocks. — Exquisite wild flowers. — The summit of the Furka. — A descent to the Rhone glacier. — Into the ice. — Swiss villages. — Brieg. — The convent inn. — The bare little chapel on the hill. — To Martigny.

WHEN we forget the scene before our dazzled eyes as we stepped out upon the balcony of the hotel Bellevue at Lucerne, earth will have passed away. There lay the fair lake, the emerald hills rising from its blue depths on every side, save where the queer old town sweeps around its curve, or beyond Pilatus, where the chain is broken, and a strip of level land lies along the water's edge, sprinkled with red-roofed farm-houses set in the midst of grain-fields, and with rows of tall, straight poplars extending to the water. This sight of peaceful homes among the heavonly hills is like a vision of earth in mid-heaven. Beyond, above, overlapping each other, rise these delectable hills. No earthly air envelops them. No earthly feet tread their fair summits. Upon the highest, among the eternal snows, rest the clouds. Truly, the heavens declare the glory of God; but Switzerland showeth his handiwork!

Beautiful was the lake in the hazy morning light, when the hills cast purple and green shadows over its bosom, when the breeze rippled its surface, and the path in the wake of the little steamer widened into an endless way; beautiful in the glare of the noonday sun, when a veil of mist half hid the far-off mountains, and the water gleamed like molten gold; but most beautiful of all when the mountains wrapped themselves in the shadows of night, and stole away into the darkness, while upon their white, still faces shone the rays of the setting sun. Then grim Pilatus stepped forth; the moon, like a burnished globe, hung over the water, across which the little steamer ploughed silver furrows, or tiny boats, impelled by flashing oars, shot over the still surface, now near, now far away; but dim, unreal, always.

It was a place of rest to us — this city of Lucerne; the "House Beautiful," where we tarried for a time before setting out again upon our pilgrimage. We wandered about the narrow streets, visited the dingy shops full of wood carvings or ornaments cut in the many-hued crystals; strayed over the low hills behind the town, through fields set with painted shrines; paused before Thorwaldsen's Dying Lion, cut in the living rock — the grandest monument that heroes ever won; and once, in the stillness of a summer morning, sat in the cathedral and heard the angels sing, when the old organist laid his hands upon the keys. Sabbath mornings we sang the old versified psalms, and listened to the exposition of a rigid faith from the lips of a Scotch Presbyterian minister, in an old Roman Catholic church — the walls hung with pictured saints and martyrs, the high altar only partially concealed, and a company of women kneeling by the door to tell their beads. Not only rest, but Christian charity, had we found here.

Almost every one who spends any time at Lucerne ascends the Righi to see the sun rise. Accordingly, five of our number prepared to follow the universal custom. In one of the little shops of the town we found some light, straw hats, with wide rims, for which we gave the extravagant price of three cents apiece, trimming them afterwards to suit individual taste, with ribbons, soft white lawn, and even mountain ferns and grasses. We slung our wraps over our shoulders by a strap, — a most uncomfortable arrangement by the way, — discarded crinoline, brought into use the shabbiest gowns in our possession, packed hand-satchels with whatever was necessary for a night upon the mountain, and then declared ourselves ready for any disclosures of the future or the Righi.

A little steamer bore us from Lucerne to Weggis — a half hour's sail. We found Weggis to be only an insignificant village, almost pushed into the lake by the crowding mountain, and seeming to contain nothing but guides and shabby horses. As we left the steamer, the open space between the pier and the hotel facing it was crowded with tourists, waiting for or bargaining with the guides for these sorry-looking beasts. No matter of what age, sex, or condition in life you may be, if you visit Switzerland, you will make, at least one, equestrian attempt; but in truth, there is nothing to fear for even the most inexperienced, as a guide usually leads each horse. The saddles for the use of ladies are provided with a rail upon one side, and the nature of the paths are such, that it would be impossible to go beyond a walk. The only danger is from over-fatigue in descending the rocky, slippery way, often like flights of stairs; then, exhausted from trying to hold back in the saddle, dizzy from gazing into frightful depths, one might easily become unseated.

When our guides were secured, one dejected beast after another was led to the wooden steps, always provided for mounting and dismounting; we climbed to our several elevations with some inward quaking, fell into line, — for single file is the invariable rule, — and passed out of the village by immediately beginning the ascent, describing, in our saddles every known curve and angle, as the path became more and more rough and precipitous. For guides we had a man with a rakish air, and — we judged from his gait — a wooden leg, who tragically wrung the perspiration from his red flannel shirt at intervals; a boy, with one of those open countenances only saved from complete lateral division by the merciful interposition of the ears, and a wizen-faced old man of so feeble an appearance as to excite my constant sympathy, since his place chanced to be by my side. He assured me continually that he was not tired, though before half of the three hours of the ascent had passed, his pale face belied his words. He was quite ready to converse, but I could with difficulty understand his English. We had paused at a wayside shed to rest the horses, and offer some refreshment to the guides, when I addressed him with, —

"What is that you are drinking? Is it goat's milk?"

"Noo, leddy," was his reply. "It is coo's;" at the same time, and with the utmost simplicity and good will, offering me the glass from which he had been drinking, that I might taste and judge for myself.

It is nearly nine miles to the summit, or Righi-Kulm. The bridle-path is rocky, rough, and steep, with a grassy slope upon either side, sprinkled at this season with dandelions, blue-bells, and odd yellow butter-cups. Often this slope changed to a precipice, still smiling with flowers. Upon every level spot orchards of pear trees and apricots had been planted, while evergreens and shrubs innumerable clung to the mountain sides, or sprang from among the rocks.

Tossed about wherever they could find a resting-place, were great boulders of pudding-stone, overhanging the path, rising in our way, or rolling in broken masses under the horses' feet. Sometimes, perched upon a natural terrace, was a *châlet*, sheltered from sweep of wind or avalanche by overhanging rocks half covered with ivy and dainty clematis. Occasionally a beggar barred the way with outstretched hand, or offered for sale some worthless trinket, as an excuse for asking alms. We hugged the rocks upon one side, as other lines of tourists wound down to meet us, upon horseback or afoot with alpenstocks to aid their steps. Peasants, laden like beasts of burden, passed as we paused to rest, with trunks, provisions, and even the red tiles for the new hotel above, strapped upon their backs, or resting there on wooden frames. They came and went; but ever present were the wonderful glimpses of earth, and sky, and shimmering lake far down below.

At the half-way house we turn to climb a gentle slope upon the mountain face. On either side the land spreads out smooth and green. It had been hot below. The air strikes us here with an icy chill. A party of young Englishmen in knickerbockers, with blue veils tied about their hats, lean over the railing of the piazza, and scan us as we pass. A Spaniard, with his dark-faced wife, step out of the path — all manner of oily words dropping from their lips. We reach the Righi-Staffel. Suddenly, upon one side, the land falls away. Among the reverberating hills echoes the *jödel*, and from a terrace far below, where a herd of dun cows are feeding, rises the tinkle of sweet-toned bells. From every path — and there are many now — winds a slow procession. The grassy slopes are all alive with people; the hotel piazza, as we pass, is crowded with travellers. Still they pour in from every side. Still the mountain-peak rises above us as we go on joining other trains, and leading others in turn. We pass through a rough gateway, ascend the broken rocks that rise like steps, follow again the narrow path, and reach at last the hotel, just before which rises the Kulm.

Talk of the solitude of nature! It is not found among these mountain peaks, grand though they are.

We dismounted in the midst of a noisy crowd. Exclamations in seemingly every known tongue echoed about us, as one party after another arrived to swell the confusion. The hill before us swarmed with tourists, who had come, like ourselves, to see the sun rise. The hotel, and even the adjoining house into which the former overflows, were more than full. Since we had taken the precaution to telegraph, — for telegraphic communication is held with most of these mountain resorts, — some show of civility awaited us. A single room was given to the four ladies of our party, where, a few hours later, we disposed ourselves as best we could. It was only a rough place, with bare plastered walls, and unpainted wooden floor; but we were not disposed to be fastidious. Dropping our satchels, we hastened up the hill before the house. It fell in a precipice upon the other side — to what frightful depth I know not. Down below, the hills spread out like level land, with lakes where every valley should be, and villages, like white dots only, upon the universal green, among which the River Reuss wound like a silver thread. But above and over all, against the sky, rose the mountains — the Bernese Alps, like alabaster walls, the gates of which, flung back, would open heavenward.

We wandered over the hillocks, which make up the summit, until the sun was gone. Gradually the darkness gathered — a thickening of the shadows until they seemed almost tangible. There was no flame of gold and crimson where the sun had disappeared; there were no clouds to reflect the warm yellow light that hung about the west. But when the night wrapped us in, the little lakes down below gleamed out like stars.

The crowd that pushed and fairly wedged itself into the *salle à manger*, when dinner was announced at eight o'clock, was quite beyond belief or computation. Everybody was tired, hungry, and impatient, after the ride to the summit. For once, silver was at a discount. One of the waiters was finally bribed to give us a private room, and slyly edged our party into a pantry, where he brought us, at immense intervals, a spoonful of soup and a hot plate apiece, after which, his resources utterly failing, he acknowledged that he could do no more. The second *table d'hôte* was served between the hours of ten and eleven at night, and consisted of numerous courses, with a similarity of flavor, suggesting one universal saucepan.

It was midnight when we finally gained our rooms, and threw ourselves upon the uncomfortable beds. The linen was wet, rather than damp. The only covering consisted of a single blanket, and the *duvet* or down pillow, always found upon the foot of continental beds.

We imagined that the sun would appear with the very earliest known worm, and at least an hour before the most ambitious lark, and dared not close our eyes, lest they should not open in time to greet him. At last, however, sleep overpowered our fears. Katie's voice roused us.

"It is three o'clock," she said, " and growing light, and I believe people are hurrying up the hill."

Profane persons should avoid the Righi; it is a place of terrible temptation. "Good heavens!" we responded, " what kind of a sun can it be to rise at such an hour?"

Our room was upon the ground floor. We pushed open the shutters and peered out, facing an untimely Gabriel, just raising to his lips an Alpine horn some six feet in length. Evidently the hour had arrived. We thrust our feet into our boots, tied our hats under our chins, and ran out to join a most ridiculous collection of animated scarecrows like ourselves. Frowsy, sleepy, cross, and caring nothing whatever for the sun, moon, or stars, we stood like a company of Bedlamites, ankle deep in the wet grass upon the summit. No sun of irreproachable moral character and well-regulated habits would appear at such an hour, we knew. The light strengthened with our impatience. Every half-closed eye was fixed upon that corner of the heavens from which the sun would sally forth. The golden gates had opened. A red banner floated out. Tiny clouds on either side awaited his coming, dressed in crimson and yellow livery. Every one of us stood upon tiptoe — the heels of our unbuttoned boots thereupon dropping down. One collarless tourist, in whose outward adorning suspenders played a conspicuous part, gravely opened his guide-book, found the place with some difficulty, and buried his head in the pages, to assure himself that everything was proceeding according to Murray. Suddenly the white faces of the distant mountains grew purple with a rage which we all shared; the flaming banner streamed out across the east, and the king of day, with most majestic step, but frightfully swollen, tell-tale countenance, rose in the heavens. I am sure he had been out all night.

The light grew clearer now. The mountains rose reluctantly, and shook off their wrappings of mist.

"Frowsy, sleepy, cross, and caring nothing whatever for the sun, moon, or stars, we stood like a company of Bedlamites, ankle deep in the wet grass upon the summit." Page 176.

The little clouds doffed their crimson finery. The man held together by the marvellous complication of shoulder-straps, closed his guide-book with an air of entire satisfaction. Evidently the programme, as laid down by Murray, had been accurately carried out. Everybody exclaimed, "Wonderful!" in his or her native tongue. All the knickerbockers, and woollen shirts, and lank water-proofs, without any back hair to speak of, trotted off down the hill to be metamorphosed into human beings, and prepare for breakfast, even to the individual who had been stalking about in a white bed blanket, with a striped border — though printed notices in every room expressly forbade the using of bed blankets as morning wraps.

When breakfast was over, there was nothing to do but to make the descent to Weggis, and return to Lucerne.

After a time, when weariness could no longer be made an excuse for lingering, we prepared for a tour through Switzerland. Engaging carriages to meet us at Fluellen, we embarked for the last time upon the beautiful lake, winding in and out its intricate ways, shut in by the towering cliffs that closed before us, only to re-open, revealing new charms as we rounded some promontory, and the lake widened again. Upon the bays thus formed, villages lean against the mountain-side. Where the rocks fall abruptly to the water, an occasional *châlet* is perched upon some natural terrace, in the midst of an orchard or scanty garden. As we touched at these lake villages, brown-faced girls, in scant blue petticoats and black bodices, and with faded hair braided in their necks, offered us fruits — apricots and cherries — in pretty, rustic baskets.

12

One of these green spots, high among the rocks, forms a sloping meadow, touching the water at last. It is an oasis in the surrounding desert of barren rock. Do you know why the grass is greener here than elsewhere? why the sun bestows its kisses more warmly? why the foliage upon the scattered walnut and chestnut trees is thicker, darker, than upon those on other mountain-sides? It is because this is Grütlii — the birthplace of Swiss liberty. Here, more than five hundred years ago, the three confederates met at night to plan the throwing off of the Austrian yoke.

Not far from Grütlii, resting apparently upon the water, at the base of one of these cliffs, is what appears at first sight to be a pretty green and white summerhouse, open towards the lake. It is Tell's Chapel, built upon a shelf of rock, and only approachable from the water. Here — so the story runs — William Tell sprang ashore, and escaped the tyrant Gessler. We sweep around this promontory and gain the last bay where lies Fluellen — a ragged village, swarming with tourists, vetturinos, and diligences. Among the carriages we find our own. It is a roomy landau, luxuriously lined with scarlet velvet, drawn by three horses which wear tinkling bells, and is capable of carrying six passengers. The top is thrown back, but a kind of calash-shade screens from the sun the occupants of what we should call the driver's seat. Our driver's place is a narrow board behind the horses. One crack of a long whip, and we are off at a rattling pace over the hard road, smooth as a floor.

For the first day we are to follow the pass of St. Gothard — that well-travelled highway which leads through mountain defiles into Italy. We dashed by Altorf, where the family of Queen Victoria's husband originated, passing the open square in which William Tell shot the apple from the head of his son. An old man is watering a horse at the basin of the stone fountain which marks the spot where the father stood. All this valley is sacred to the memory of William Tell. In a village near by he was born; in the mountain stream, just beyond, he is said to have lost his life in the attempt to save a drowning child. After Altorf, the road winds among the meadows, though the mountains rise on every side, with *châlets* perched upon points which seem inaccessible, so steep are their sides. It is haying time, and men and women are at work in the fields and upon the mountain-sides, carefully securing every blade of grass. Once, when we had begun to wind up the mountains, where a grass-grown precipice fell almost sheer to the valley below, a girl clung to its side, and pulled with one hand the grass from between the rocks, thrusting it into a bag that hung about her neck. She paused to gaze after us as we dashed by, a kind of dull awe that never rose to envy lighting her face for an instant. O, the hungry, pitiful faces of these dwellers upon the heights! the pinched, starved faces of the little ones especially, who forgot to smile — how they haunted us! At noon we sweep up to the post-house at Amsteg, with a jingle of bells, a crack of the whip, and an annunciatory shout from the driver. There is no village that we can see. The piazza of the post-house is filled with travellers, lunching before a long table; half a dozen waiting carriages stand in the open space before it; as many hostlers, with knit caps upon their heads, from which hang long, bright-colored tassels, are busy among the horses. At a short distance the Reuss River rushes past the house; upon its bank is a little shop, with its store of Swiss curiosities and trinkets. A couple of girls fill a tray with the dainty wares, and cross the space to tempt us. One has a scarlet handkerchief knotted under her handsome, dark face. She turns her brown cheek to her shoulder, tossing a word back as the young hostlers contrive to stand in her way.

One by one the carriages take up their loads and go on. We soon follow and overtake them, winding slowly up among the rocks, which seem ready to fall upon us. We form a long train, a strange procession, bound by no tie but that of common humanity. The meadows and soft, green mountain-slopes are left behind as we ascend, crossing from one side to the other by arched bridges thrown over the chasm, at the foot of which foams the torrent. Higher and higher rise the rent rocks — bare, black walls, seamed, and scarred, and riven, their summits reaching to the sky. They close about us, shutting out everything of earth and heaven, save a narrow strip of blue far above all. Even the sweet light of day departs, and a gloom and darkness as of a brooding tempest falls upon us as the way narrows. Suddenly a mad, foaming torrent, with angry roar, leaps from the rocks above, to toss, and writhe, and moan upon the rocks below the arch upon which we stand. The water rushes over them, and dashes against them. It swirls, and pants, and foams, while high above it all we stand, our faces wet with the spray, our ears deafened by the terrible roar. Truly, this *is* "The Devil's Bridge."

Think of armies meeting here, as they did in the old Napoleonic wars, contending for the passage of the bridge below. Think of the shrieks of the wounded and dying, mingling with the raging of the waters. Think of the white foam surging red among the rocks; of the angry torrent beating out the ebbing life of those who checked its flow. Think of the meeting of hosts in mortal conflict where no eye but God's could witness it, upon which not even bird or startled beast looked down. It was like a dreadful dream from which we passed — as through deep sleep — by a way cut in the solid rock out into God's world again. Still, from one side of the road rose the rocks that began to show signs of scanty vegetation now; from the other fell the precipice to the torrent. We had left the carriages at the bridge, and singly or in companies toiled up the road that doubled back upon itself continually. Often we climbed from one of these windings to the next above, by paths among the rocks, leaving the carriages to make the turn and follow more slowly. Often our way was the bed of a last year's torrent, or our feet touched the borders of the stream, as we pulled ourselves up by the shrubs that grew among the rocks. The ice-chill in the air brought strength for the time, and perfect exhilaration. It seemed as if we could go on forever, scaling these mountain heights.

At last the carriages overtake us, and we reluctantly resume our places. The road is built out upon the mountain-side. It offers no protection against the fall of the precipice. It narrows here. We look down, and say, "How dreadful a careless driver might make this place!" and, shuddering, draw back. Suddenly the train pauses, and down the long hill runs a shout, "A carriage has gone over." We spring out, and run to the front. "Is any one killed?" "No; thank God, no one is harmed." We gather upon the edge of the precipice. Upon the rocks below lies the body of a horse — dead, with his fore feet raised, as though pawing the air; and mingling with the white waters, and tossed about in the raging stream, are the shattered remains of a carriage and its contents.

It seems that two young men from Canton Zurich essayed to make a tour of the mountains with their own horse and carriage — a foolhardy experiment, since none but tried horses, used to these passes, are considered safe here. All went well, however, until they reached this point, where a torrent falls down the mountain-side to the road, under which it passes with a fearful noise. It might, indeed, startle the strongest nerves. The horse, young and high-spirited, shied to the edge of the precipice, then reared high in the air. They saw that he must go over when his fore feet came down, and springing out, barely escaped a similar fate. We all passed the spot with some trepidation, the most of us preferring to walk; but our horses, accustomed to the road, were utterly unmoved by the swooping torrent. At night we reached Andermatt — only an untidy little village, lying in one of these upper valleys, bustling and all alive around the door of its one inn; but how green and beautiful were the mountains, shutting us in all around, after the desolation through which much of our way had led! Upon the side of the nearest was a triangular patch of wood-land, — firs and spruces, — said to divide and break the force of the avalanches that sweep down here in the spring. It can be nothing but a story of what had been true formerly, when the wood was more extensive. Down these mountains, as night closed in, straggled a herd of goats to the milking, tinkling countless little bells, while the roar of the Reuss, which we had followed until it was now hardly more than a mountain brook, mingled with our dreams as it ran noisily through the village.

On we went the next morning, wrapping ourselves warmly, for the air was chill as November, though at Lucerne, only twenty-four hours before, we had suffered a torrid heat. Just beyond Andermatt, at Hospenthal, we left the St. Gothard, to follow the Furka pass. All around was barren desolation, as we went on, **still ascending**, leaving every sign of human life behind. Rocky and black the mountains rose, bearing only lichens and ferns. Occasional patches of snow appeared, lying in the beds of the last year's torrents, or scattered along beside the road. But here, where Nature had bestowed little to soften and beautify, she had spread upon the barren land, and tucked in among the rocks, a covering of exquisitely delicate flowers. You cannot realize, until you have seen them, the variety, beauty, and profusion of the Alpine flowers. Looking back in memory upon the bare rocks, doomed to stand here through all time in solitude and in the midst of desolation, as though in expiation of some sin, it is pleasant to remember that at their **feet and** in their clefts these little flowers nestle and bloom.

We gathered nosegays and made snowballs, and at noon gained the summit of the Furka, and rested an hour or two at the inn — the only sign of house or hut we had seen since morning. The rough *salons*, the passage, the doorway, even the space outside, were alive with tourists. It is a continual jar upon one's sense of the fitness of things, something to which you never become thoroughly accustomed, until all freshness of sight-seeing is passed — this coming suddenly upon the world in the midst of the unutterable solitude of nature; this plunging into a crowd dressed in the latest style, and discussing universal frivolities where the very rocks and hills seem to stand in silent adoration. But after the first moment you, too, form one of the frivolous throng, the sight and sound of which shock the sensibilities of the next comer.

From the inn a **tongue of** land, green and dotted with flowers, falls into the valley below. On either side rises a mountain, scarred by the torrents dried away now, and stained this day with the last year's snow, while beyond — ever beyond, like some heavenly heights we vainly strove to gain — rose the Bernese **Alps**.

From the summit of the Furka we descended to the Rhone glacier by one of the zigzag mountain roads. Looking down over the edge, we could see below, the ways we were yet to follow on the mountain face before accomplishing the descent. The horses dashed down at a flying pace. The inclination of the road was not sufficient to alarm; but the turns are always so frightfully abrupt as to make it seem as though the leader must dash off. But no; he invariably swung around just upon the outer edge, held, it seemed sometimes, by the traces, and with a crack of the driver's whip was off again before our fears, if we had any, could find words.

One of these abrupt turns fairly hangs over the glacier, where the icy river has fallen into broken masses from a higher point, before spreading out in the narrow valley just here where it ends. Only a short distance from the foot of the glacier is the inn, with its scattered out-buildings, where we were to spend the night. The sheer descent from the summit of the Furka is only about half a mile; but though our horses had galloped the whole distance, and the inn was in sight all the time, we were three hours reaching it; so many turns did the road make upon the face of the mountain.

It was a gloomy valley, shut in by mountains, and surrounded by lesser hills all soaked and dripping with icy streams that chilled the air. We gained the foot of the glacier from the inn by a rough path over and among the rocks, and stones, and heaps of gravel it had brought down and deposited here. From beneath the solid mass of ice flowed a hundred shallow streams, which, uniting, form the beginning of the River Rhone. We penetrated for a short distance the gallery cut into the glacier, surrounded and shut down upon by the walls and ceiling, of a deep blue color, and were preceded by an old man, who awoke the echoes by uttering a series of broken cries. What with the echoes and horrible chill, the place seemed most unearthly, and we were glad to retreat.

The roar of torrents, and hardly less thunderous noise of departing diligences, awakened us the next morning. We were soon off upon the road, skirting the mountains, rolling through the pleasant valleys, and passing village after village now. They seemed silent and deserted, their occupants perhaps busy in the fields, or serving at the inns, or among the mountains as guides. One was a mass of ruins, thrown down in the bed of a torrent, among which a few dull-faced peasants were at work, with a hopeless, aimless air, that promised little. A mountain stream, swollen to a flood by melting snows, had swept it away in a night.

At noon we lunched at Viesch — a slipshod, unwashed village, by the side of the young Rhone, which so far, in its dirty, chalk-white color, was not unlike the white-headed children that played upon its banks. Some of the party left the horses to their noon rest, and strayed out upon the road beyond the village. On its outskirts was a fine new church, of stone. If only something of its beauty could but come into the everyday lives of the poor people here! We sat down upon the steps to wait. Across the road was an orchard, roughly fenced in; beside it one of the picturesque Swiss peasant houses — all steps, and queer old galleries, from which a little tow-headed girl stared out at us in open-eyed wonder, as we blew the down from the dried dandelions we had pulled along the way, and questioned if, in our far-off homes, our mothers wanted us!

It seemed as though we could descend no farther; and yet, after sweeping through a valley, a sudden turn would disclose another, far below, to which this was as a mountain. So down we sped the whole day long; once by a frightfully-narrow zigzag road, the worst by far of any we had seen; passing still through the villages so charming in the distance, but dirty, and full of odors by no means pleasing, as we drew near. At night we rattled into the paved square before the inn at Brieg, just as the first drops of a coming shower wet its stones.

This was evidently something more than a village. The houses were plastered, instead of being of wood with a rich, burnt-sienna color, like those we had seen along the road through the day. They were thickly clustered together, and from their midst rose the four turrets of a chateau. Our inn was a delightfully-dingy old place. It had been an Ursuline convent, and abounded in queer, dark passages, rough stone stairways, and old wooden galleries overlooking the square. One of our rooms had been a part of the convent chapel, and was still lighted by a window just beneath the groined roof. Here we braided our hair, and knotted our ribbons, and dreamed, in the twilight that followed the rain, of the hopeless ones who had sought comfort in other days within these walls, and fell asleep at last, knowing full well that the fringe of many an old prayer was still caught and held in the arches high over our heads. We walked up through the town the next morning, to the beginning of the Simplon Pass. Somewhere in the narrow sreets we passed the old chateau, and pressed our faces against the bars of a gate, in order to gain some idea as to the domestic economy of the family which had bestowed upon Brieg its air of importance. But the chateau had degenerated into a brewery, and the court-yard was filled with old carts, clumsy and broken.

Farther up the hill the door of a little chapel stood invitingly open, waiting for stray worshippers, or a chance-burdened heart (for even so far away as Brieg, hearts do grow heavy, I doubt not). Something in its narrow, whitewashed poverty touched our sympathies. It is rare indeed in these countries to find a chapel without at least some votive offering to make it beautiful in the eyes of the simple people: here was only a crucifix, and we pleased ourselves with the fancy that when the ships come in that we sent out as children — laden with hopes that were to be bartered for treasures — we would return, and hang the walls with pictures, and make the whole place wonderful in the eyes that had seen only its bareness. The shower the night before had laid the dust, and the drive that morning was most enjoyable. Following the course of the noisy Rhone, we reached Sierre at noon, where we left the carriages with regret, and took the railway train to Martigny.

CHAPTER XIV.

AMONG THE EVERLASTING HILLS.

The quaint inn. — The Falls of the Sallenches, and the Gorge de Trient. — Shopping in a Swiss village. — A mule ride to Chamouni. — Peculiarities of the animals. — Entrance to the village. — Egyptian mummies lifted from the mules. — Rainy days. — Chamois. — The Mer de Glace. — "Look out of your window." — Mont Blanc. — Sallenches. — A diligence ride to Geneva. — Our little old woman. — The clownish peasant. — The fork in the road. — "Adieu."

OUR hotel here at Martigny, was even more suggestive of romance than the one at Brieg. It had been a monastery, and was an old, yellow-washed structure facing the street, with a rambling garden surrounded by high walls, clinging to it in the rear. Low, dark rooms, with bare, unpainted floors, like the waves of the sea in smoothness, were given to some of our party, while Mrs. K. and I were consigned again, with singular appropriateness, to what had been the chapel. Its windows overlooked the straggling, half-dead trees, and bare, hard-baked earth of the open space before the door, which was always being crossed by strings of mules ornamented with bright saddle-cloths, and still further with the ubiquitous tourist arrayed in every known costume of the period. Village girls, too, passed under the trees, knitting as they went, and horrible creatures afflicted with the *goître* — that curse of this region — which we met at every turn now.

To gain the long, low refectory where we dined, or to pass from one room to another, necessitated crossing the brick-paved cloisters, upon which all the doors of the second story opened. Here a row of columns encircled a narrow, inner court-yard — so narrow as to be nothing more than a slit in the walls, yet wide enough to allow the shimmering sunlight to drop down upon the vines twined around the columns, and light the whole dingy interior into a weird, strange beauty.

We rode out to the Falls of the Sallenches, — one of the mist veils left hanging from many of these Swiss mountains by the water-sprites, — and penetrated the Gorge de Trient upon the shaky gallery that follows its windings; wandered about and beyond the town; stole into an old church, and brought away the memory of a lovely virgin face; and haunted the dingy shops in the vain hope of making a few necessary purchases. These shops were not unlike our New England country stores in their combined odors and confused incapabilities. Behind the counters, or more likely sitting in the doorway with the inevitable blue knitting in hand, were old women, of hard, baked-apple faces, whose ideas of the luxuries of a woman's wardrobe were so far below what we considered its necessaries, that we parted in mutual surprise, to say the least, and without gain on either side.

Sabbath morning, English church service was held in the parlor of one of the hotels; after which a clergyman in gown and bands **discoursed from the text**, "And there shall be no more sea," — a peculiarly comforting hope to some of us.

Monday morning, we mounted the horses and mules waiting in dejected impatience before the door, and started upon the long ride of twenty-two miles to Chamouni by the Tête Noir Pass. A wide, pleasant avenue, shaded by walnut trees, led out of the town; after which we began to ascend the gently-sloping mountain-sides, passing occasional villages, and besieged by beggars and venders of fruit, as usual. Indeed, these beggars are so constant in their attendance and importunity that one forgets to mention them, unless recalling flies and similar swarming annoyances.

The scenery, as we went on, was often grand, always interesting; the sky overcast, but at times the clouds, drifting apart, disclosed peaks or "needles" so far above the mountains about us as to seem a revelation of heaven. The path was treacherous and rough — skirting precipices, descending in rocky steps or slippery mire, and crossing mountain streams by narrow, insecure bridges. Single file is the invariable rule in all these mountain excursions, and after a time **the isolations** of this mode of travelling adds to its wearisomeness. Solitude is delightful; but as some one has said, "How pleasant it is to have a friend near by to whom you may remark, 'How delightful is solitude!'"

As you follow the windings of the narrow, steep path, you have a choice between addressing the back of the one who precedes you, and throwing a remark over your shoulder to those who come after. Involuntarily you fall to studying the curves **of the** former, and are utterly indifferent to the fact that the latter are probably meditating upon the intricacies of your back hair. Mule-riding is conducive to grace of neither soul nor body; still you know you are not making such a spectacle of yourself as did the woman just passed — who twisted about in the saddle as though worked along by rotary motion. Perhaps not.

As you leave the villages to plunge into the woods, the flies swarm like beggars; and it is only when the guides have cut boughs from the trees, which you wave before you, wickedly suggesting palm branches, that you can proceed with tolerable comfort, and without the fear of an unexpected toss in the air, as one kick after another runs down the line.

Each horse or mule has his own slight peculiarities of habit and disposition. I recall one whose inordinate curiosity led him to walk always upon the verge of the precipices, so that the rider's feet overhung the frightful depths. Murray says it is best to allow these animals to choose their own paths. But to hang suspended between heaven and earth at the mercy of a strap and a mule, will shake one's faith, even in Murray.

My horse this day was possessed of the dreamy, melancholy nature of a poet, with the attendant lack of ambition. Every time we wound funereally through a village, he would walk deliberately to the mounting-steps, and wait most suggestively. Indeed, an air of abstraction characterized all his movements; even when, as we approached these villages, raising his head, he would seem to sniff the odors of Araby the Blest; which was a mistake, a delusion of his fancy shared by none of the others of the party. That he was without pride I must confess. No stable did we pass so poor, none so mean, that he was ashamed to pause and offer to enter with meek obdurateness.

Poetic as was his temperament, his appetites were developed in a remarkable degree. Once upon a narrow bridge we met two walking haystacks, out from which peered great, blue eyes. If the size of his mouth had corresponded at all to his desires, they would have vanished from sight in a twinkling; as it was, they barely escaped. Whether or not insatiable thirst is an attribute of a poet, I do not know; but each stream which crossed the path, — and the whole country seemed liquidizing, — each drinking-trough beside the way, — and to my excited imagination they seemed to form an unbroken line, — was an irresistible temptation. It was only by shouting, "Yeep! Yeep!" in staccato chorus, and vigorously applying the palm branches, thus engaging his attention and diverting his thoughts into less watery channels, that we succeeded in making any progress whatever. Under this disciplinary process his nature was at last so far subdued that he would have passed the ocean itself without a sigh, I am sure.

There was a rest of an hour at the Tête Noir inn at noon, shut in by the firs, and rocks, and mountains, then we went on to Argentière, where we gladly exchanged the horses and mules for some low, open carts with a couple of villagers in blue blouses for drivers. In these we accomplished the remaining three or four miles, and made a triumphal entry into Chamouni.

It was late in the afternoon when we crawled up the narrow, thronged street to the Hôtel Royal, from which the English, French, and American flags were flying. The clouds had dropped lower and lower, until a fine mist was beginning to deepen into rain, and the guides and tourists detained in the village fairly jostled each other at the intersection of the two principal streets, which seemed to form the village Exchange. The mire of the streets was thickly stamped with hoof-prints and the marks from the nails that stud the shoe-soles of the mountain climbers. Line after line of doleful looking objects, which might prove Egyptian mummies when unwrapped, were being lifted from still more sorry looking beasts before the door of the hotel, and assaying to mount the steps, with a stiffness and angularity of movement in which we all sympathized.

Indeed, after dinner, when a bright fire was lighted in the long *salon* where the various parties gathered to read, write, look over stereoscopic views, or chat among themselves, it was amusing, as well as pitiable to observe the abortive attempts at ease and flexibility as these individuals crossed the polished floor, to hear the groans smothered to sighs as they resumed their seats. "Mules!" whispered the girls, nudging each other, and mindful of the delight which misery is said to find in company.

All the next day the rain dripped down upon the village from the heavy clouds that hid the mountains. Everybody improved the opportunity to write letters, or yawned over the books scattered about the *salon*. Among them was a well-thumbed copy of "Artemus Ward, His Book." At the foot of each page the local allusions of the jokes were explained, I remember. Out in the street, umbrellas were dodging about from one shop to another. These rainy days, though a loss to the guides, are harvest times for the shopkeepers. Photographs and stereoscopic views of the mountains, the glaciers, and daring climbers hanging on by their eyelids, abound here, with any amount of wood and chamois (?) horn carving and crystal ornaments. Speaking of chamois-horn, if you expect to see in Switzerland — as you do in geographies — chamois perched upon every crag, preparatory to bounding from peak to peak, you will be grievously disappointed. Not a chamois will greet your eyes. We passed — I have forgotten where — a pen in which, by paying a certain sum, we might look upon a veritable live chamois; but we had no desire to see the incarnation of liberty thus degraded.

We waited two days for the uplifting of the clouds, making, in the mean time, an excursion up the Montanvert to overlook the Mer de Glace — which is not a sea, but a river of ice, like all the glaciers that have worked themselves down into these valleys. We retired one night with the cloud curtains spread low over our heads; the next morning a voice from outside of our door called, "Look out of your window." We sprang up, seized the cord of the shutters, and behold! a new heaven and new earth! Every vestige of cloud was gone. The mountains were bathed in sunlight, vivid green were the peaks before us, which had never met our gaze until now, while behind the nearest, against the deep blue of the summer sky, rose the three vast white steps which lead heavenward, the highest of which men call Mont Blanc. All that morning, as we descended from the valley of Chamouni to Sallenches, we turned continually to look back; and still, white and beautiful, but growing less in the distance, rose the triple domes.

We had taken a carriage to Sallenches: here we find places in the open diligence for Geneva. We pause in the first village through which we pass, where a knot of people gathers about a round little old woman. She wears a wide-rimmed hat over her neat frilled cap, and carries another upon her arm. Her waist is dimly defined by the strings of a voluminous apron, and her mind entirely distracted by the cares attendant upon the disposal of a cotton bag, a wicker basket, an old umbrella, and a box, which half a dozen men seize upon with clumsy hands, in good-natured officiousness, and thrust into the baggage compartment, while the women and children press about her, kissing the rough, ruddy cheeks, and uttering what we are sure must be blessings — odds and ends of which float up to us. Evidently the little, old woman is going a journey. Aided by a dozen rough, helpful hands, she climbs the ladder to her place beside us, with a deprecatory though cheerful "*Bon jour*" to us all, subsiding into a corner, where she is immediately submerged as her belongings are showered down upon her; last of all a crumpled letter is tossed into her lap.

The driver mounts to his place; she leans over; a perfect gust of blessings, and kisses, and adieus follow us, as with a crack of the whip the horses spring away, and we leave the village far behind.

Suddenly — for we have turned away our faces — the little old woman's hand is plunged into the cotton bag under our feet. We venture to look around. The tears have gone; her face beams like the sun, as she brings

"Evidently the little old woman is going a journey." Page 196.

out of the depths a couple of eggs. Another dive, and she emerges with a piece of bread. A pinch of salt is added from the basket, and her breakfast is complete. She hospitably offers a share to each of us. We decline; and as a shadow dims the brightness of her face, Katie adds quickly, —

"We have had two breakfasts already."

The little old woman rolls her round, blue eyes to heaven, with a pious ejaculation. Such lavish extravagance is beyond her comprehension.

"That is like you rich people," she says. "We are only too happy if the good God sends us one." And she relapses into a wondering silence.

"Does madame travel far?" we venture presently.

"Ah, yes." And she shakes her head slowly. Words cannot express the distance, it is so great.

"But she has been this way before?" we go on.

"No, never before." And again the round, blue eyes seek heaven, and again a deep sigh follows the words. She has finished her lunch, and, diving under our feet, emerges after a time with a box, which, opened, discloses a small store of peppermints. This she offers with some hesitation, and we each hasten to accept one, her countenance beaming more and more as they disappear. "Given to hospitality," the little old woman has been, we know.

When the box is with difficulty replaced, the string of the bag drawn, the basket arranged to her satisfaction, the umbrella placed at a pleasing angle, she balances herself upon the edge of the seat, and glances fearfully from side to side as we swing along the smooth road. Once, when the wheel passes over a stone, she seems to murmur a prayer.

"Madame is not afraid?" we say.

"O, very much. These diligences are most dangerous." And now she is glancing over her shoulder at a rocky wall of mountains which follows the road at a distance. "They might fall." And she shudders with the thought. We assure her that it is impossible; but she has heard of a rock falling upon a diligence, and thinks it was upon this road. And all the horror of the fearful catastrophe is depicted upon her face. Gradually we learn that the little old woman has never travelled in a diligence before; that she has never before made any journey, in fact. For forty years she has kept the house of the *curé* in her native village. Now, she tells us with a sigh, and uplifted eyes, he has "become dead," and she is obliged to seek a home elsewhere among strangers. Here she turns away her eyes, which grow dim as her smile, and for a moment forgets her fears.

We are approaching a village. She hastily searches her basket and brings out the crumpled letter which had been thrown into her lap. As we dart through the narrow street and across an open square, she leans out, utters a word in a sharp, excited tone, and, to our surprise, throws the letter far out into the dust of the street. An idle lounger in the square starts at her voice, runs heavily across the street, and picks it up. She sinks back, all cheerful smiles again. She has chanced upon the very man to whom the letter was addressed.

The dust rolls up from the great wheels. She exchanges the hat upon her head for the one over her arm, covering the former carefully with a corner of her apron. This, she tells us, as she arranges the second upon her head, she was accustomed to wear when she picked vegetables of a morning in the garden of the good *curé*. And the sighs return with the recollection of her master.

The day wears on with heat and sifting dust. By and by, at another village, a filthy, dull-faced peasant clambers up the ladder and stumbles into a vacant place. We shrink away from him in disgust. Our little old woman only furtively draws aside her neat petticoats. Soon she engages him in conversation. We see her lean far forward with intense, questioning gaze upon the distance where he points with dirt-begrimed finger. Then with a sigh which seems to come from the baggage compartment beneath us, so very deep and long-drawn it is, she turns to us. She, too, points to a range of hills, very dark and gloomy now, for they are covered with woods, and the shadow of a cloud lies upon them.

"It is there, beyond the mountains, I am going;" and the shadow of the cloud has fallen upon her face. All the sunshine has faded out of it. Then, with something warmer, brighter than any sunshine gleaming in her eyes, she adds, "But the good God takes care of us wherever we go."

We have reached a fork in the road. There is no village, no house even, in sight. Why, then, do we pause? The ladder is raised.

"It must be for me!" gasps the little old woman, casting one bewildered glance over to where the shadows are creeping, and then calmly gathering together her possessions. We grasp the hands she extends, we pour out confused, unintelligible blessings. Is it the dust which blinds our eyes? Even the clownish peasant stumbles down the ladder, and lifts out her box. The driver remounts. The whip cracks. We lean far out. We wave our hands. Again the dust fills our eyes so that our sight for a moment is dim, as we dash away, leaving her sitting there alone upon her box, where the two roads meet. But beyond the hills where the shadows rested, we know that the sun still shines for our little old woman whose master "became dead."

CHAPTER XV.

LAST DAYS IN SWITZERLAND.

Geneva. — Calvin and jewelry. — Up Lake Leman. — Ouchy and Lausanne. — " Sweet Clarens." — Chillon. — Freyburg. — Sight-seers. — The Last Judgment. — Berne and its bears. — — The town like a story. — The Lake of Thun. — Interlaken. — Over the Wengern Alp. — The Falls of Giessbach. — The Brunig Pass. — Lucerne again.

WE dashed up to the hotel upon one of the fine quays at Geneva, and descended from the open diligence with all the appearance of travellers who had crossed a sandy desert. There is an air of experienced travel which only dust can impart.

The most charming sight in the city, to us, was our own names upon the waiting letters here. In truth, there are no sights in Geneva. Tourists visit the city because they have been or are going elsewhere, beyond. If they pause, it is to rest or buy the jewelry so far-famed. To be sure the view from almost any window opening upon the blue Rhone is pleasing, crossed by various bridges as it is, one of which touches Rousseau's Island. But our heads by this time were as full of views as that of a Boston woman.

Calvinists and Arminians alike visit the Cathedral, and sit for a moment in the old reformer's chair, or at least look upon the canopy of carved wood from beneath which he used to preach. There are few monuments here. The interior is bare, and boarded into the stiff pews, which belong by right and the fitness of things, not to these grand, Gothic cathedrals, but to the Puritan meeting-houses, where we gather less to breathe a prayer than to sit solemnly apart and listen to a denunciation of each other's sins.

It is a little remarkable that the city where Calvin made and enforced such rigid laws against luxury and the vanities of the world should, in these latter days, be noted for the manufacture of jewelry. But so it is; and to walk the streets and gaze in at the shop windows would turn the head of any but the strongest-minded woman. Two or three addresses had been given us of manufactories where we could be served at more reasonable rates than at the grand shops. We climbed flight after flight of dingy stone stairs, in dingier buildings, to reach them, and found ourselves at last in little dark rooms, almost filled by a counter, a desk, and a safe or two. Certainly no one would think of looking for beautiful things here! But we had become tolerably accustomed to such places in Paris, and were not at all surprised when one shallow drawer after another was produced from behind the counter, and a blaze of gems and bewildering show of delicately executed gold work met our eyes. If you care for a *souvenir* only, there are pretty little finger-rings encircled by blue forget-me-nots in enamel, which are a specialty of Geneva. But if you possess the means and disposition, you may gratify the most extravagant desires, and rival Solomon in magnificence.

Twice a day steamers leave Geneva to ascend the lake. It was a bright, summer afternoon when we embarked from the pier beyond our hotel, and steamed away past the villages that lie along its edge. Among them is Coppet, the home of Madame de Staël, the towers of which rise up behind the town. The deck of the steamer was alive with tourists. One party, from meeting at every turn, rests even yet in memory; the ladies stout, red-faced, and showily dressed, with immense "charms" pendent from their *chatelaines* — shovels, tongs, and pokers, *life-size* — the result of a sojourn at Geneva, doubtless.

For some time after leaving the city, we could look back upon Mont Blanc, white and beautiful, rising above the dark mountains, and lying close against the sky blue as the waters of the lake. The likeness of a recumbent figure of Napoleon — the head and shoulders alone, — in the garb of a grenadier was startling, haunting us even after it had changed again to a snow-white mountain. As though the hero slept, like those in German legends, until his country called him to awake and lead its hosts to battle.

At Ouchy we leave the steamer, where the gardens of the grand hotel Beaurivage come down to meet us. How delightful are these Swiss hotels! with their pleasant gardens, many balconies, wide windows, and the flying flags outside; and within, scrupulous neatness, and even elegant appointments. The rooms vary in size rather than in degree of comfort, there being none of the sudden leaps or plunges between luxury and utter discomfort, found in so many hotels — elsewhere. The floors are bare, the strips of wood forming squares or diamonds, waxed, and highly polished. A rug here and there invites bare feet. A couple of neatly-spread beds stand foot to foot upon one side of the room, sometimes with silk or lace coverlets, but with always the *duvet*, or large down pillow, at the foot. There is no stint of toilet arrangements. A lounge and easy-chairs tempt to idleness and repose; and a round table, of generous proportions, awaits the chocolate, rolls, fresh butter, and amber honey, when the last curl is in order, the last ribbon knotted, and you have rung for your breakfast. Of course the rooms vary in degree of ornamentation. The walls are often beautifully tinted or frescoed, and the furniture elegant; but the neatness and comfort among these summer hotels are almost universal. Sometimes, in one corner, or built into the wall, stands the high, white porcelain stove, so like a stray monument that has forgotten its inscription, and is sacred to many memories; and the long, plate-glass windows, swinging back, open often upon a balcony and a charming view. No wonder that half the hotels in Switzerland are named *Bellevue*.

An omnibus bears you from Ouchy, which is simply the port of Lausanne, back into the city, past pretty country residences, walled in, over the gates of which the owners have placed suggestive names: "My Rest;" "Heart's Desire;" "Good Luck;" "Beautiful Situation;" anything which fancy or individual taste may dictate. Of Lausanne I recall little but an endless mounting and descending of stairs. The city is built upon a hill, intersected by ravines, which accounts for this peculiar method of gaining many streets from others above and below. We made but a hurried visit. It was market day, and ugly women, old and young, were sitting upon the sidewalks in the narrow streets, knitting, with the yarn held over the fore-finger of the left hand, and selling fruits and vegetables between times. In the honey market the air fairly buzzed and swarmed; yet still these women knit, and gossiped, and bargained complacently, unmindful of the bees in their bonnets. From Ouchy we made an excursion to the head of the lake. It is a short voyage of two hours to Villeneuve, the last town. Clouds hid the distant mountains; but those lesser and nearer, upon our right, as we went on, were bare, and broken, and rocky, contrasting strangely with the gently swelling slopes upon the other side, covered with vineyards, and with quiet little villages at their feet. Each of these villages has its romantic association; or, failing in that, a grand hotel to attract summer visitors. Vevay boasts the largest hotel, but nothing more. Just beyond Vevay is "Clarens, sweet Clarens," the willows of which dip into the lake. Here, if Rousseau and Byron are to be believed, Love was born; possibly in some one of the mean little houses which border the narrow streets.

Soon after leaving Clarens, the gray, stained tower of Chillon rises from the water, near enough to the shore to be reached by a bridge. With the "little isle" and its three tall trees marked by the prisoner as he paced his lonely cell, ends the romance of the lake. Poets have sung its beauties, but Lucerne had stolen away our hearts, and we gazed upon the rocks, and vineyards, and villages, with cold, critical eyes. It was only later, when the summer twilight fell as we lingered upon the balcony before our windows at

Ouchy that we acknowledged its charm. The witching sound of music came up from the garden below. Upon the silver lake before us, the lateen sails, like the white wings of great sea-birds, gleamed out from the darkness; the tiny wavelets rippled and plashed softly against the breakwater; and where the clouds had parted overhead, a horned moon hung low in the sky, while the mountains resolved themselves into shadows or other waiting clouds.

There was a little church between Ouchy and Lausanne, gained by crossing the fields, where we remembered the Sabbath day, and joined in the church service led by an English clergyman. These Sabbaths are like green spots now in memory, — restful, cool, refreshing, and pleasant to recall, — when the world, and all haste and perplexity of strange sights, and sounds, and ways, were rolled off like a heavy burden, while we gathered, a little company of strangers in a strange land, yet of one family, to unite in the familiar prayers, and hymns, and grand old chants.

Monday morning the "American cars" bore us away from Lausanne to Freyburg. But such a caricature are they upon our railway carriages, that we were inclined to resent the appellation. Low, bare, box-like, with only three or four seats upon each side, they hardly suggested the original.

We had chosen the route through Freyburg that we might visit the suspension bridge, and hear the celebrated organ. The city clings to the sides of a ravine after the perverse manner of cities, instead of spreading itself out comfortably upon level land. So steep is the declivity that the roofs of some of the houses form the pavement for the street above. At the foot of the ravine flows a river crossed by bridges, and the towns-people have for centuries descended from the summit on one side to climb to that upon the other, until some humane individual planned and perfected this suspension bridge, — the longest in the world save one, — which is thrown across the chasm. In order to test its strength, when completed, the inhabitants of the city, or a portion of them, gathered in a mass, with artillery and horses, *and stood upon it!* Then they marched over it, preceded by a band of music, with all the dignitaries of the town at the head of the column. Since it did not bend or break beneath their weight, it is deemed entirely safe.

Through the most closely-built portion of the city runs the old city wall, with its high, cone-capped watch-towers, and the narrow, crooked, and often steep streets are very quaint. The sense of satisfaction which returns with the memory of these streets is perhaps partly due to the fact, that the girls of the party surveyed them from above great squares of gingerbread bought at a *pâtisserie* near the station, and ate as they strolled through the town over the pavings of these crooked ways. The bread of dependence is said to be exceedingly bitter; but the gingerbread of Freyburg is uncommonly sweet, in memory.

When the suspension bridge has been crossed and commented upon, every one strikes a bee-line to the Cathedral, which rises conspicuously above its surroundings. It would be very amusing to watch the professional sight-seers at all these places, if one did not belong to the fraternity, which makes of it quite another affair. There is no air of pleasuring about them; no placid expression of content and sweet-to-do-nothing. They seldom are found meandering along the tortuous streets, the milk of human kindness moistening every feature, beams of satisfaction irradiating every countenance. They never spend long hours wandering among the cloisters of old cathedrals, or dream away days by storied shrines, as friends at home, who read of these places, fondly imagine. By no means. The sight-seer is a man of business. He has undertaken a certain amount of work, to be done in a given time. He will do or die. And since it is a serious matter, involving doubt, he wears an appropriately solemn and preoccupied expression of countenance. He darts from point to point. He climbs stairs as though impatient Fame waited for him at the top. His emotions of wonder, admiration, or delight, must bestir themselves. He drives to the first point of interest, strikes a bee-line to the second, cuts every corner between that and the third, and then, consulting his watch, desires to know if there is anything more, and experiences his only moment of satisfaction when the reply is in the negative. And the most remarkable part of all is, that he goes abroad to enjoy himself.

But even if one is less ambitious, if you are so fortunate as to be naturally indolent, and to delight to dwell in the shadow of dreams, you will shake off dull sloth here. You live and move in a bustling crowd. Every storied spot is thronged with visitors. Far from musing by yourself, you can at best but follow in the wake of the crowd, with the drone of an endless story from the lips of a stupid guide in your ears, bringing only confusion and weariness.

A notice upon the door of the Cathedral informed us that the organ would not be played until evening. We held a council of war, and decided to go on. Just over our heads, as we stood before the entrance, was a representation of the Last Judgment, cut in the stone, in which the good, very scantily attired, and of most self-satisfied countenances, trotted off after St. Peter, who carried the father of all keys, to the door of a castle representing heaven, while the poor wicked were borne away in a Swiss basket, strapped upon the back of a pig-headed devil, to a great pot over a blazing fire, which a little imp was vigorously blowing up with a pair of bellows. The wicked seeming to outnumber the good (this was designed many centuries ago), and the pot not being large enough to hold them all, the surplus were thrust into the jaws of a patient crocodile near by. Seated in an arm-chair, above all this, the devil looked down with an expression of entire satisfaction.

The interior of the Cathedral was in no way remarkable. In the choir (which you know, perhaps, is not a place where girls stand in their best bonnets to sing on Sundays, but the corner of these great cathedrals in which the church service is held) were some fine stained glass windows; but even here, horrible monkeys and hideous animal figures, life-size, were cut from the wood, and made to stand or crouch above the stalls where the priests sit. Those old ecclesiastic artists must have believed in a personal devil, who assumed many forms.

A threatened shower hastened our steps to the station some time before the arrival of the train, which seemed to come and go without regard to the hour appointed. While waiting, we read the advertisements framed and hanging upon the walls, of hotels, shops, &c. One of the latter, in a triumph of English, ran, —

WOOD CARWINGS;
CHOOSE AS NOWHERE ELSE.

We reached Berne before night, and drove to the Hotel ——. If it could by some happy chance have been turned inside out, how comfortable we might have been! The exterior was most inviting. A German waiter of Irish face, who had a polyglot manner of speech, difficult to be understood, showed us to our rooms; and the *table d'hôte*, to which we descended an hour later, was made up of an uncommon array of prim-visaged individuals. Dickens's Mr. Chadband, in a very stiff, white neckcloth, was my *vis-à-vis*. I looked every moment for his lips to open, and — " Wherefore air we gathered here, my friends?" to issue forth.

The guide-book had informed us that the greatest attraction of Berne to strangers was the fine view of the Bernese Alps to be gained from here; but a curtain of cloud hung before them during all our stay. Still we were interested in the queer old city, with the second story of the houses, through many of the streets, projecting over the sidewalk, forming gloomy arcades, and bright red cushions in the window seats, where pretty girls sat and sewed, and watched the passers down below. I remember it rained, and there was a market held out in the square before the hotel windows in the early morning, where the umbrellas made every old woman to dwell in her own tent for the time. When it was over, and the rain had ceased to fall, we waited in front of the old clock-tower before driving out through the pleasant suburbs, with market women, baskets on their arms, stray children, idle loungers, and alert tourists, for the feeble puppet-show heralded by the asthmatic crow of a rheumatic cock. Of course it was a procession of bears. Everything in Berne is, or has to do with, a bear, since the city was founded upon the spot where somebody killed a bear. Bears surmount most of the stone fountains in the streets; they ornament the monuments erected to heroes. Cut from wood, they are offered for sale as *souvenirs;* stuffed, they are exhibited at the zoölogical gardens; and, to crown all, government supports in luxury a whole family of bruins. We left the carriage upon the Nydeck bridge, to look down into the immense circular basin where they are kept. It must be a dull life, even for a bear. They are ugly creatures, with reddish fur, and spend their time climbing a leafless semblance of a tree, with no object but to descend again, or in sitting up to beg for biscuits of visitors. So universal has the custom of begging become in Switzerland, that even the bears take to it quite naturally.

The mountains obstinately refusing to appear, we left Berne for Thun, passing through a lovely country. Only occasionally did a road appear; then it would seem to extend for long miles, bordered by immense, close-planted trees. Neither fences nor hedges were there to divide the fields; but patches of grain were thrown down anywhere and at any angle. Potatoes were sown like grass instead of being planted in hills, and were devoured this year by rot — the worst feature in the landscape. All through the early summer we had seen hemp growing everywhere. Now it was cut, and lying outspread upon the ground in odd regularity, an occasional head only being left to run to seed.

There was nothing to visit in Thun. But the whole town is like a story. Not an elegant, high-toned story, to be sure, though a picturesque old castle and church lifted themselves aristocratically above the more humble town. The streets are narrow, and as picturesque as they are dirty, with a sidewalk sometimes above the first, low, projecting story of the houses.

It is a mile from the town to the lake of the same name. Close by the steamer landing, where we were to embark for Newhaus, is the hotel Bellevue. Within the garden enclosure were several little *châlets;* one to serve as reading-room, another as *salle à manger*, while a third, beyond the pond, where swan were sailing, displayed Swiss wares for sale. Here we lunched and rested for an hour, before going up the lake. It is a voyage of an hour and a half to its head, past beautifull villas upon one side, and precipitous rocks upon the other. Once landed at Newhaus, — where there was not a *new house* that we could see, but only a scanty collection of little huts, — we searched about, with the mud ankle deep, among the crowd of waiting vehicles, for the omnibus which was to bear us the two miles and a half to Interlaken and the hotel Jung Frau. If you recall your geography lessons, you will perhaps know that the two lakes, Thun and Brienz, are separated by a strip of land, upon which is this village of Interlaken. It is hardly more than one long street, with green fields and a row of trees upon one side, and a line of houses standing back upon the other. In full view from the windows of these summer hotels, when the sky is clear, rises the Jung Frau, between two great mountain peaks. This is the only *sight* in Interlaken, and yet the town throngs with visitors. It must be intolerably hot here at times, lying low among the mountains as does this valley. In the fields, behind the grand hotels, is a long, low Kursaal, a rustic affair, with a wide piazza. You may lunch, and read the newspapers; but government has prohibited the gambling. There are delightful excursions to be made from here, which accounts, perhaps, for the crowded hotels. And there are several fine shops, where you may buy all or any of the curiosities for which the country is well known.

A rainy day crowded these shops and the hotel parlors, and made a busy scene the length of the street, which is very like a country road. But the second morning after our arrival, we rose early, to prepare for an excursion over the Wengern Alp. The Jung Frau, hidden the day before, appeared in full view with the rolling away of the clouds, and we desired to approach nearer to the shy maiden. All the listlessness of the day before was past. As we stepped out of the little *châlet*, in the hotel garden, where — the hotel being full — we had slept in a room only vacated for the night, with a pair of immense red slippers behind the door, and Madame's gowns hanging from pegs on the wall, everybody was astir. More than one party was sipping their scalding coffee as we entered the hotel breakfast-room, while, under the great trees outside, guides and saddled horses waited impatiently.

When we had tied on our wide-rimmed hats, and gathered our shawls, we found a roomy carriage, an open landau, waiting for us at the side-door of the hotel. We drove quickly out of the town, followed by and following other carriages, until we formed a long procession by the time we had reached the valley of Lauterbrunnen and began the ascent. It is a deep, dark valley, shut in by innumerable overhanging rocks, from which thread-like waterfalls hang suspended in air, or are lost in spray. Hardly does the sun seem to penetrate its depth, and an indescribable gloom, as well as chill, pervades the place. From a few scattered cottages women and children emerged to follow the carriages, begging mutely or offering fruits, while at one point a man awaited our approach to awake the echoes with an Alpine horn.

After an hour we reach Lauterbrunnen, and leave the carriage at the door of an inn, where a crowd bargains and waits for guides and horses. We swell the number. When we are served, we mount to our places, and file out of the straggling village, turning before we reach the Staubach Falls — a stream of silvery spray that never touches earth, but swings and waves in mid-air. The ascent grows more and more steep. The recent rain has added to the icy streams, which filter constantly from snows above, and the horses sink in the mire, or slide and slip in a way by no means reassuring. Often the path is mounted by steps of slippery logs; when added to this is a precipice upon one side, we hold our breath — and pass in safety. We commend each other as we perform feats of valor and intrepidity which would make our fortune in the ring, we fancy.

The guides, insolent and careless, stroll on in advance, leaving the most timid to their **own** devices. Presently, as we enter a perfect slough of despond, we see a man before us scraping the mire with a hoe vigorously, as we come in sight.

" You should give this poor man something," says one of the guides. " He keeps the road in order." I wish you might have seen the *orderly* road!

Suddenly we gain a point where the land spreads out into green knolls before us and on either side — a strip of almost level verdure, with, on one hand, peak **on** peak, rising till they touch heaven; upon the other, the Jung Frau, draped in snow. It seems so near, so very near, — though the land drops between us and it into a deep ravine, and the snow-clad peaks and needles are a mile away, — I almost thought I might guide my horse **to** the verge of the chasm, and reaching out, gather the **snow** in my hand. Across the summit, the clouds, white as itself, drifted constantly, hiding it completely at times. It had been a tiresome climb of two hours and a half, and we were glad to rest an hour before descending. As we turned the corner of the Jung Frau inn, having dismounted from our horses, **we were met** by our ubiquitous, stout friends of Lake Leman memory, to whom, I presume, we seemed equally omnipresent. *Table d'hôte* was served here, one party following another, until the long table was full. Occasionally the noise of an avalanche, like the sound of distant thunder, aroused and startled us, and caused us to vacate every seat. But though the mountain appeared to be so near, these avalanches, which sweep with tremendous force, carrying tons of ice and snow, seen from this distance, seemed like nothing more than tiny mountain streams let loose.

From the inn, we mounted and went on half a mile, before reaching the summit and beginning the uncomfortable descent. We thought every bad place must be the worst, as the horses slid down the slippery stones, or descended the log steps with a peculiar jerky motion, suggesting imminent and unpleasant possibilities. But, after fording torrents swollen by the rain, crossing narrow, treacherous bridges, sliding down inclined planes, and whole flights of stairs, the guides informed us that we should reach a *dangerous place* presently!

When, finally, we came to it, we were quite willing to dismount, and make our way down over the rocks for a mile, trusting to our own feet, and beset continually by women and children, who appeared most unexpectedly at every turn, to thrust little baskets of fruit or flowers into our hands. The very youngest child toddled after us with a withered field-flower, if nothing more. So early do they begin to learn the trade of a lifetime.

We entered Grindelwald late in the afternoon. The shadows of night, which fall earlier in these valleys than elsewhere, were already gathering. The few, scattered cottages, walled in by the everlasting hills, with the snow-covered Wetterhorn in full view, and the glacier behind it, wore a cheerless and gloomy air in the quick-coming twilight. Train after train of tourists, upon horses and mules, or dragging weary feet, descended from among the mountains, to find carriages here and hasten away. Only these arrivals and departures gave a momentry life to the spot. What must it be when the summer sun and the last visitor have left it?

We, too, sought out our waiting carriage, and rolled away in the summer twilight, down the beautiful road, wide and smooth enough to lead to more dreadful places than the pleasant valley of Interlaken, where, for a day at least, was our home.

The next afternoon, instead of spending the Sabbath here, we decided to go on to Giessbach, on the Lake of Brienz, to visit the celebrated falls. We had rested comfortably in the hope of a quiet day in the little *châlet*, where more permanent arrangements had been made for our disposal. But the enterprising member of the party, to whom we owed not a little, in a happy moment of leisure, gave herself to the study of the guide-book, the result of which was — Giessbach. We gathered our personal effects together, under the pressure of great excitement and limited time, reached the little steamer, fairly breathless, and then sat and waited half an hour for it to move. It was not, however, a tedious time; for there occurred an incident which engaged our attention.

"What do you suppose they're going to do with that calf?" asked the boy of the party, who, like all boys, was of an inquiring turn of mind. "They've got him into the water, and are poking him with sticks."

Upon this we all became immensely interested. A calf had fallen into the water, between the pier and the steamer; but the fruitless efforts made by everybody, interested or disinterested, were to rescue, not drown, the creature, as a bystander would have inferred. Suddenly, as his own struggles carried him away from the wharf, and he was about to sink, a white, delicate hand, bound with rings, and an arm daintily draped, were thrust out from one of the cabin windows, seized upon the head disappearing in a final *bob*, and held on until assistance came, when the poor animal, half dead with fright, was drawn from the water.

At last the steamer moved away from the wharf, and in an hour or less the little pier at Giessbach received us. There is a tiny valley, one hotel, and a series of pretty cascades here. But all these are reached by a smooth road, winding back upon itself continually, and so steep that carriages do not ascend it. You must walk, or rather climb it, for twenty minutes, or accept the disagreeable alternative of being carried up by two men in a chair, resting on poles. The day was warm; our arms were weighed down with satchels, &c.; but we pressed on, while, commenting upon our personal peculiarities in dress, gait, and general air, as they looked down upon us from the height we almost despaired of gaining, were the complacent, comfortable souls, who always reach these desirable places the day before any one else, and, in the freshest possible toilets, sit, like Mordecai, in the gates.

It may have been droll to them; it was a most serious matter to us. It was Saturday afternoon, and each one felt and acted upon the realized necessity of outstripping his neighbor, in order to secure rooms. Finally the gentlemen hastened on, our ambition failing with our strength, and we were happy in finding comfortable quarters awaiting us when we had gained the hotel at last.

It was the most delightful little **nook** imaginable when we were rested and refreshed. Until **then it possessed** no charms in our **eyes.** It is a little valley, high above the lake, towards which it opens, but shut in on three sides by precipitous hills. Down the face of **one the** cascades fall. Back against another the **hotel is built, facing the lake;** its *dépendance*, and the inevitable shops for the sale of Swiss wood-carving and crystals, being ranged along the third side. The **whole** place is not larger than a flower-garden of moderate **size.**

We were served at our meals by pretty, red-cheeked girls, in charming Swiss costumes; and when we **had** been out after dark to see the falls illuminated in different colors, while the rustic bridges, which span the cascades at various heights, were crossed by these picturesque figures, I felt as if we were all part of **a** travelling show, for whom this dear little level spot was the stage, and that a vast audience waited outside, where the walls of hills opened upon the lake, for the curtain to fall. It was like the Happy Valley of Rasselas, which we left with regret when the peaceful Sabbath was over.

Across the lake, **at Brienz,** Monday morning, a carriage waited to bear us on, over the Brunig Pass, into the clouds and out again; then down, down, past village, and lake, and towering hills, resting again at Sarnen, then on to Lucerne, into which we swept, with tinkling bells and cracking whip, to find the city gay **with** streaming flags and flowery arches, erected for **some** singing *fête,* but which to us were all signs of a happy welcoming.

CHAPTER XVI.

BACK TO PARIS ALONE.

Coming home. — The breaking up of the party. — We start for **Paris** alone. — Basle, and a search for a hotel. — The twilight ride. — The shopkeeper whose wits had gone "a wool-gathering." — " Two tickets for Paris." — What can be the matter now ? — Michel Angelo's Moses. — Paris at midnight. — The kind *commissionaire*. — The good French gentleman, and his fussy little wife. — A search for Miss H.'s. — " Come up, **come up**." — " Can women travel through Europe alone ? " — **A word** about a woman's outfit.

TO dash through the town, along the quay where we had walked so many times beneath the trees or leaning over the low parapet fed the fishes, past the two-spired cathedral, the cloisters of which had become so familiar, to mount the hill and draw up before the door of the Bellevue again, welcomed by the innkeeper, and greeted with outstretched hands by "Charles," who had served our chocolate, while familiar faces met us at every window or upon the stairs, to pull up the shutters, **throw wide** open the windows, and drink in the glorious beauty of the scene before our eyes — all this was delightful, but fleeting, like all earthly joys, and mixed with pain; for here we were to say "good by."

Our pleasant party was to break up. The friends

in whose care we had been so long, were off for Germany, and Mrs. K. and I must turn our faces towards home. We were to renew our early and brief experience in travelling alone. It had been as limited as our French, which consisted principally of "*Est-ce que vous avez?*" followed by a pantomimic display that would have done credit to a professional, and "*Quel est le prix?*" succeeded by the blankest amazement, since we could seldom, if ever, understand a reply.

"Are you afraid?" queried our friends.

"No; O, no." The state of our minds transcended fear.

It was a hot day when we took our last view of the lake, as we rode down the hill from the hotel, past the cathedral, past the shaded promenade upon the quay, to the station; but we heeded neither the heat nor the landscape when we were once in the train and on the way. Our hearts were heavy with grief at parting from friends, our spirits weighed down by nameless fears. It was a wicked world, we suddenly remembered. Wolves in sheep's clothing doubtless awaited us at every turn. Roaring lions guarded every station. We clutched our travelling-bags, umbrellas, and wraps, with a grasp only attained by grim fate or lone women. Gradually, however, as the uneventful hours wore away, we forgot that in eternal vigilance lay our safety, and relaxed our hold.

We had left Lucerne at noon; at five o'clock we reached Basle. Here we were to spend the night at the hotel *Les Trois Rois*. Every step of the way to Paris had been made plain to us by our kind friends.

"Let me see; the hotel is close by the station?"

queried Mrs. K., when we had left our trunks, as our friends had advised, and followed the crowd to the sidewalk.

"Yes," I replied with assurance, "close by, they said; I am sure."

Accordingly we turned away from the long line of hotel omnibuses backed up against the curb-stone, to the fine hotels on each side of the straight avenue, extending as far as the eye could see. Alas! among their blazing names was no "*Trois Rois.*" We read them over and over again. We even tried to pronounce them. Not a king was there, to say nothing of *three.*

In a kind of bewilderment we strayed down the avenue. Might not some one of the fair dwellings gleaming out from the shrubbery prove the house we sought? There was a rattle and clatter behind us; a passing omnibus. Another, and still another followed. Serene faces beamed out upon our perplexity. A cloud of dust enveloped us as the last rolled cheerfully by, upon the end of which we read, with staring eyes, "*Les Trois Rois.*"

"Ah!" gasped Mrs. K.

"Sure enough," I replied.

"Why, suppose we take it?" said she, slowly.

"Suppose we do," I assented, with equal deliberation. But by this time the little red omnibus was a speck in the distance.

"At least we can follow it." And we quickened our steps, when, with almost human perversity, it turned a distant corner, and vanished from sight.

Fixing our eyes steadily upon the point of disappearance, we hastened on, and on, and on! I have a faint recollection of green trees, of stately houses, of an immense fountain swaying its white arms in the distance — mirage-like, for we never approached it; of the sun pouring its fierce rays upon us as we toiled on, with our wraps and satchels turning to lead in our arms.

We reached the corner at last. There was no omnibus; no hotel in sight; only the meeting of half a dozen narrow, crooked streets, crowded with carriages, and alive with humanity. All settled purpose left us then; our wits, never very firmly attached, followed. We became completely demoralized.

"Suppose you inquire," suggested Mrs. K., after a period of inaction, during which we were pushed, and jostled, and trampled under foot by the crowd.

If I possessed one capability above another, it was that of asking questions, especially in a strange language. Upon this corner where we were standing, rose an imposing building, in the open doorway of which stood a portly gentleman, with a countenance like the setting sun, in glow and warmth. A heavy mane flowed over his shoulders. Evidently this was the first of the roaring lions! Taking our lives in our hands, we approached him.

"Do you speak English?" I ventured.

"*Nein*," was his reply, with a shrug of the leonine shoulders.

I drew a long breath and began again.

"*Parlez-vous Français?*"

His reply to this was as singular as unprecedented. He turned his back and disappeared up the wide stairs in the rear.

"This *may* be foreign politeness," I was beginning, doubtfully, when he reappeared, accompanied by an intensified counterpart of himself. The setting sun in the face of this man gave promise of a scorching day.

"*Parlez-vous Français, monsieur?*" I began again, when we had bowed and "*bonjour*"-ed for some time.

"*Oui, oui, mademoiselle.*"

Here was an unexpected dilemma. A terrible pause ensued. Then, with an effort which in some minds would have produced a poem at least, I attempted to make known the object of our quest. I cannot begin to tell of the facial contortions which accompanied this sentence, nor of the ineffable peace which followed its conclusion. It made no manner of difference that his reply was a jargon of unintelligible sounds. Virtue is its own reward. One sentence alone I caught, as the indistinguishable tones flew by. We were to take the first street, and then turn to the right.

"What did he say?" asked Mrs. K., when we had *merci*-d ourselves out of their radiant presences.

I explained the direction we were to follow.

"Horrible countenance he had," she remarked, as we pursued our way.

"O, dreadful," I assented.

"Nobody knows where he may send us," she continued.

Sure enough! In our alarm we stopped short in the street, and stared at each other with horrified countenances.

"I have heard — " I began.

"Yes; and so have I," she went on, shaking her head, and expressing by that gesture most fearful possibilities.

A bright thought seized me. "He told us to turn to the *right;* we will turn to the *left!*" And with that happy, womanly instinct, said to transcend all judgment, *we did.* Strange as it may appear, though we went on for a long half hour, no "*Trois Rois*" gladdened our eyes.

Suddenly Mrs. K. struck an attitude. "A fine appearance we shall present," said she; "two lone women, dusty and heated, our arms full of baggage, straggling up to a hotel two mortal hours after the arrival of the train. We'll take a carriage."

To me this inglorious advent was so distant in prospect that it held no terrors, nothing of mortification even. "*Les Trois Rois*" had become a myth, an idea towards which we vainly struggled.

"If it were only across the street," she went on, rising to the occasion and warming with the subject, "we would go in a carriage."

One approached at that moment. We motioned to it *à la Mandarin*, with our heads, our hands and arms being full. The driver raised his whip and pointed solemnly into the distance. We turned to gaze, seeing nothing but the heavens in that direction. When we looked back, he was gone. We should not like to affirm — we hardly dare suggest — we are sure of nothing but that he vanished from before our eyes.

A second appeared in the distance. We began in time. We pawed the air wildly with our umbrellas. The very satchels and wraps upon our arms nodded and beckoned. In serene unconsciousness the driver held to his course.

"Well!" I exclaimed, indignantly.

"I should think so," added Mrs. K., with emphasis.

"Is there anything peculiar, anything unusual in our personal appearance?" I asked, glancing down upon our dusty appointments. As we concentrated our energies and belongings for one final effort, a benignant countenance smiled out upon us from above a *cipher*. We were storming a private carriage!

The third attempt was more successful. The driver paused. We requested him, in English, to take us to "The Three Kings." He only stared and shook his head. We tried him with "*Les Trois Rois.*" He seemed still more mystified.

"What can be done with people who do not understand their own language!" I exclaimed in despair.

We tried it again with our purest Parisian accent. An inkling of our meaning pierced his dull understanding. He rolled heavily down from his seat, and opened the door with the usual "*Oui, oui.*" We entered and were driven away.

"Do you think he understood you?" queried Mrs. K.

"No-o."

"Well, where do you suppose he will take us?"

"I don't know, and I don't much care," I responded, in desperation.

We settled back upon the cushions. The peace that follows resignation possessed our souls. O, the luxury of that jolting, rattling ride, as we wound in and out among the tortuous streets! A full half hour passed before the dusky old hotel darkened above us, surmounted by "The Three Kings" arrayed in Eastern magnificence, and wearing gilded crowns upon their heads.

Fate had been propitious. This was our destination, without doubt, though we had made a grand mistake as to its location. We descended at the entrance with the air, I trust, of being equal to the occasion. We calmly surveyed the assembled porters, who hastened to seize our satchels aud wraps. We demanded a room, and inquired the hour of *table d'hôte*, as though **we** had done the same thing a thousand times before. Mrs. K. was right; there was a moral support in that blessed carriage.

Table d'hôte over, we strayed into a pretty **salon** opening from the *salle à manger*. Both were crowded — over doors and windows, and within cabinets filling every niche and corner — with quaint specimens of pottery — pitchers, vases, and jars, ancient enough in appearance to have graced the domestic establishment of the original "Three Kings." The glass doors thrown back **enticed us** upon a long, low balcony, almost swept by the rushing river below — the beautiful Rhine hastening on to its hills and vineyards. We leaned **over**, smitten with **sudden** homesickness, and sent a message back to Rolandseck of happy memory.

With the faint shadows of coming twilight **we** wandered out into the square before the hotel. A line of *voitures* extended down one side, every one of which **was** quickened into life at our approach. We paused, with foot upon the step of the first, for the *carte* always proffered, upon which is the number of the driver and the established rate of fares. He only touched his shiny hat and prepared to gather up his reins.

"O, dear!" we said; "this will **never do**; **we must**

not go." And we stepped down. The porters upon the hotel steps began to cast inquiring glances. One or two stray passers added their mite of curiosity, when the knight-errant, who always breaks a lance for distressed womanhood, appeared upon the scene. We recognized him at once, though his armor was only a suit of gray tweed, and he wore a fashionable round-topped hat for a casque.

Almost before we knew it, we were seated in the carriage, the *carte* in our hands, and were slowly crawling out of the square — for a subdued snail-pace is the highest point of speed attained by these public vehicles.

The memory of Basle is as shadowy, dim, delightful, as was that twilight ride. Where we were going, we neither knew nor cared; nor, later, where we had been. We wound in and out the close streets of the old part of the city, full of a busy life so far removed from our own, that it seemed a show, a picture; below the surface we could not penetrate. We rolled along wide avenues where the houses on either side were white as the dust under the wheels. Once in a quiet square, we paused before an old *Hôtel de Ville*, frescoed in warm, rich colors. Again upon the outskirts of the city, before a monument; but whether it had been erected to hero or saint I cannot now recall. And somewhere, when the dusk was deepening, we found an old church, gray as the shadows enveloping it, with a horseman, spear in hand, cut in *bas relief* upon one side. What dragon he made tilt against in the darkness we never knew.

Even our driver seemed to warm beneath the influences which subdued and dissipated our cares. He nodded gently and complacently to acquaintances, eliciting greetings in return, in which we, in a measure, shared. He hummed a guttural, though cheerful song, which found an echo in our hearts. He stood up in his place to point the way to misguided strangers, in whose perplexities we could so well sympathize. And once, having laid down the reins, and paused in our slow advance, he held a long and seemingly enjoyable conversation with a passing friend. To all this we made no manner of objection, rather we entered into the spirit of the hour, and were filled with a complacency which was hastily banished upon our return to the hotel, where, as we put into the hand of our benevolent driver his due, and the generous *pour boire* which gave always such a twinge to our temperance principles, he demanded more.

"He claims," said the porter, who was assisting our descent, "that he has been driving with the carriage lamps lighted. There is an extra charge for that."

"But he left his seat to light them this moment, just before we turned into the square," we replied, indignantly.

The porter shrugged his shoulders. That is the end of an argument. There is never anything more to be said. We submitted at once, though our faith in benevolent humanity went to the winds.

Somewhat dispirited, we climbed the stairs to our room. "One day more," we said, "and our troubles will be at an end." But, alas! one day was as a thousand years!

It was to be an all-day's ride to Paris, from nine

o'clock in the morning until half past nine or ten at night. So, while waiting for breakfast, we hastened out into the town, in search of a bookstore, and something to while away the dull hours before us.

A young man, of preternaturally serious countenance, was removing the shutters as we entered a musty little shop. We turned over the Tauchnitz's editions of English novels until we had made a choice, the value of our purchases amounting to four or five francs, and gave him a napoleon. With profuse apologies he left us to get it changed. Returning presently, he threw the silver into a drawer, and handed the books to us, with a "*Merci.*"

"Yes," we said; "but—" Arithmetic had never been my strength; still something was clearly wrong here.

"The change," said Mrs. K. " He has given us no change." Sure enough; but still he continued to bow and thank us, evidently expecting us to go.

We tried to explain; eliciting only one of the blank stares that usually followed our attempts at explanation.

"The man must be an idiot," Mrs. K. said, gravely.

"He certainly has an imbecile expression of countenance," I assented. He stood still, bowing at intervals, while we calmly weighed and balanced his wits before his eyes. We tried signs; having through much practice developed a system to which the deaf and dumb alphabet is as nothing. We attempted to convince him that a part of the money was ours.

He smiled, and assured us, in a similar way, that the books belonged to us, the money to him.

There was so much justice in this, that **we** should **doubtless** have assented, had not his own wits finally asserted themselves. Blushing like a bashful boy, he suddenly exclaimed, counted out the change, and poured it into our hands with so many apologies, **that we** were glad to retreat.

It was a discouraging beginning for the new day. Still we would not despair. We had assured our anxious friends that we were quite able to take care of ourselves. We would triumphantly prove our own words. Breakfast over, **and** our bill settled without mishap or misunderstanding, we started for the station in the hotel omnibus, in company with a stout, genial Frenchman, who spoke a little English, and **his fussy** little wife. When we entered the station, the line formed before the ticket-window was already formidable. It lacked fifteen minutes of the hour when **the** train would start, and our baggage was — where? We **seized a** *commissionaire*, slipped a piece of money into his hand in a very bungling, shamefaced way, and, presto! in a moment our trunks appeared among the other baggage, though **we had looked** in vain for them before. Then, with a sensation of self-consciousness approaching guilt, I stepped to the foot of the line before the ticket-window.

"Two tickets for Paris," I gasped, finding myself, after a time, brought face to face with the sharp-eyed official. "What is the price?" But before I could utter the words, the reply rattled through my head like a discharge of grape-shot. Every finger resolved itself into ten, as I essayed to open my purse and count out the gold pieces. What should I do! I had not enough into ten francs; it might as well have been ten thousand! Mrs. K. was waiting at a little distance; but the place once lost in the line could not be regained, and there was our baggage yet to be weighed, and the hands of the clock frightfully near the hour of departure. There was an impatient stamping of feet behind me, as I stood for a moment dizzy, bewildered, with an angry buzz of voices ringing with the din and roar in my ears. Then I rushed down the room to Mrs. K., and explained as hastily as possible. She filled my purse, and I flew back to find the line pushed forward and my place gone. One glance at the hands of the clock, at the discouraging line of ticket-seekers yet to be served, — how could I go to the foot again! Then I walked straight to the window with the courage of despair. A low growl ran down the line, the *gendarme* on guard stepped forward, expostulating excitedly; but, blessings on the man at the head of the line, who pushed the others back, and gave me a place, and even upon the grim official behind the window, who smiled encouragement, and gave me the tickets, while the *gendarme* stormed. I stepped out again, conscious only of the wish — strong as a prayer — that we were safe again in Lucerne, or — some other place of peaceful rest.

Wedged in among the crowd, we saw one trunk after another weighed and removed, while ours remained untouched. I pulled the sleeve of a porter. My hand held my purse. The suggestion was enough. In a moment our trunks were weighed, and the little paper ticket corresponding to our "check" safe in our possession. I turned, conscientiously, to reward the porter; but we were jostled by a score of elbows, each encased in the sleeve of a blue blouse. Which was the one I sought? I could not tell. Each answered my glance of puzzled inquiry with one of expectation. Diving to the depths of my purse, I found it to contain one solitary centime — nothing more. I slipped it into the hand nearest, and from the start of surprise and delight was immediately convinced that it was the wrong man. However, it did not matter. There was no time to explain. The doors opening upon the platform, which remain locked until the last moment, were thrown open, and we hurried away, found places upon the train, and sank back upon the cushions exhausted, but happy. For ten hours at least, nothing could happen to us. The guard passed the window, examining the tickets, and slamming the doors, making our safety doubly sure. A moment more, and with a noiseless motion we were off. Hardly had the train started before it stopped again. One after another our companions left us — for we were not alone in the compartment. "Strange," we said, yet too thoroughly exhausted to be curious. It was still more strange when, after a short time, they each and all returned. They began to whisper among themselves, pointing to us. "What *can* be the matter *now?*" we queried, suddenly mindful that life is a warfare, and roused to interest.

Our fellow-travellers proceeded to enlighten us in chorus, and in the confusion of the outburst, we caught — by inspiration — at their meaning. We had crossed the frontier into France, and the baggage was examined here. We hastened out and into the station.

All the trunks but our own had been checked. With his hand upon one of these, an official demanded the key, upon our appearance. Remembering an episode in its packing, we demurred, and proffered the key of another. Already vexed by the delay, his suspicions were roused now. He demanded the key of the first, which we gave up with wicked delight. The by-standers drew near. Indeed, a crowd was the embarrassing accompaniment to all our unfortunate experiences. The official turned the key with the air of doing his duty if he perished in the attempt, when the lid flew open, and a hoop-skirt, compressed to the final degree, sprang up into his startled face, like a Jack-in-the-box. The spectators laughed — French though they were — as, very red in the face, he vainly tried to replace it, entirely forgetting to search for contraband articles.

No other incident disturbed the quiet of that long day's ride to Paris. At some queer little station we descended to lunch, and returned to our places, laden, like the spies of Eschol, with luscious grapes. Our fellow-travellers dropped out along the way, only, however, to be replaced by others. We had not succeeded in securing places in the compartment reserved for ladies alone; but the French gentlemen who were our companions proved most courteous in their polite indifference to our movements. An old gentleman among these, elicited our outspoken admiration for his grand head. We were secure in our native language, we knew.

"Lovely face!" we exclaimed, unblushingly. "What a head for a sculptor! Quite like Michel Angelo's Moses, I declare."

Before the day was over, "Michel Angelo's Moses" addressed us in excellent English.

When the darkness gathered, when the night settled down, something of its gloom oppressed us. Once safely housed in Paris, we should be at rest; but there were still difficulties to be overcome. Our friends had telegraphed to Miss H. that we should arrive by this train; but the number of her house we did not know, nor did they. We were only sure that her apartments were over the *Magasin au Printemps*. Still that was tolerably exact; we would not be uneasy. At ten o'clock at night we stepped down from the train into a confusion of tongues and elbows which I cannot describe, and followed the crowd into the baggage-room. I say *followed* — we were literally lifted from our feet and borne along. There was no baggage in sight. We waited until an hour seemed to have passed, and still no trunks appeared.

"Suppose we leave them, and send a porter from the house in the morning to find them;" and acting upon this, we struggled out of the station into the great paved square at one side. The night was dark; but the gas-lights dimly lighted up a line of carriages at the farther side, towards which we hastened, and had seated ourselves in one, when a *commissionaire* came running across the square, and putting his head in at the carriage window, asked if we had any baggage.

"Yes," we replied; but the rattling words that followed brought only confusion to us. Our minds, already overtaxed, gave way at once. It is pleasant to recall the patience and good-nature of that official. It is pleasant, when old things have so entirely passed away, to remember the Paris of 1869 as, at least, a city into which women might come at midnight, alone, unprotected, and be not only free from insult and imposition, but actually cared for, and sent to their rightful destination, in spite of their own ignorance and incompetence.

"Stay here," said our friend in uniform; and he disappeared, to return in a moment with the stout French gentleman who had been our companion in the hotel omnibus at Basle. We met with mutual surprise, and pleasure on our side at least.

"*Do* any one look for your baggage?" he asked.

"No," we replied. "We thought we might leave it."

"You must go," he said.

The *commissionaire* took possession of our check and the driver's *carte*, and I followed the two back to the station, leaving Mrs. K. to guard our satchels, &c., in the carriage.

"Wait one leetle moment," said the kind French gentleman; "I bring madame." And in a moment he dragged the fussy little woman from the crowd, handing her over with the triumphant air of having now settled all difficulties.

"Madame speak ze Eengleesh fine," he said.

Looking down from an immeasurable height, the little madam condescended to remark that their servant was looking for their baggage.

"Ah!" I responded. "Then we are not permitted to leave our trunks."

"I am sure I don't know," she replied, looking so greatly bored, not to say exhausted, that I did not think it best to press the matter. "Our servant is attending to it," she repeated.

Her husband's face fairly glowed with satisfaction while this side conversation was being carried on. Evidently he believed the whole French baggage system to have been elucidated for my benefit. I thanked him heartily, as we exchanged cordial adieus. Even the fussy little woman gathered, for the moment, sufficient life to attempt to bow; which, alas! never got beyond a stare. The *commissionaire* seized upon a blue-bloused porter, and gave me to him with the check, the *carte*, and a few sharply-spoken directions. Clinging to that blue sleeve, I was borne through the swaying, surging mass of humanity, into the baggage-room — how, I never knew. Our trunks were identified, lifted, not thrown, by my porter upon a hand-truck, which dragged for itself and us an opening in the crowd. Once out upon the platform, the porter pushed doggedly on into the darkness, though I had left Mrs. K. and the carriage in the square at one side. I expostulated. He held persistently to his course. I gave one thought to poor Mrs. K., resigned to what fate I knew not, and then, woman-like, followed my trunks.

It was all explained, when, dimly outlined in the darkness before the station, we espied a sea of shiny hats and shadowy cabs; and when, after long shouting of the number of our own, by the porter and everybody else, it finally crawled up to the steps where we were standing, Mrs. K.'s anxious face looking out of the window.

"I began to think you were lost," she said. "You can fancy my feelings when the driver gathered up the reins and drove out of that square."

We made a thank-offering upon the palm of every grimy hand, suddenly outstretched; then the driver paused, whip in the air, for the address of our destination.

"*Magasin au Printemps*, Boulevard Haussman." He stared, as everybody had, and did, along the way. If they only wouldn't! We repeated it. He conferred, in a low tone, with the man on the next box, who got down from his place, and came around to our window to look at us. One or two lounging porters joined him. The *Magasin au Printemps* is a large dry and fancy goods establishment, which had been closed, of course, for hours, since it was now nearly midnight. It was as though we had reached New York late at night, and insisted upon being driven to *Stewart's*. The little crowd stared at us solemnly, in a kind of pitiful curiosity, I fancied. I think, by this time, our countenances may have expressed incipient idiocy. We attempted to explain that Miss H.'s apartments were over the *Magasin*, and the driver mounted to his seat, though, I am obliged to confess, with an ominous shake of his head.

As we rolled out into the wide boulevards our spirits rose. The sidewalks were crowded with promenaders, the streets with carriages. The light of a glorious day seemed to have burst upon our dazzled eyes. Paris, gay, beautiful Paris, which never sleeps, was out, disporting herself.

"We will not be anxious," we said; nor were we in the least. "Even if we cannot find Miss H.'s, some hotel will take us in. Or, failing in that, we can drive about until morning."

A thought of our respective and respectable families did cross our minds with this lawless suggestion. In happy unconsciousness, they believed us still safe with our friends.

We crawled up the Boulevard Haussman. There were the closed doors and shutters of the *Magasin au Printemps*. Two or three other doors met our gaze. The driver paused before one. We descended, and pulled the bell. You must know there are no door-steps, in Paris, leading to front doors, as with us. The first floor is, almost without exception, given up to shops; and dwellings, unless pretentious enough to be houses enclosing a court-yard and entered from the street by passing through great gates, are simply apartments in the two, three, and four stories above these shops.

Some invisible mechanism swung back the great double doors as we pulled the bell, disclosing a pretty, paved court-yard, with a fountain in the centre, surrounded by pots of flowers. A glass door at one side, revealed wide marble stairs, down which a charming little portress was tripping.

"Is this Miss H.'s?" we asked in English. She only shook her head. We paraded our French. She seemed lost in thought for a moment, then, with a "*Oui, oui*," ran past us to the carriage, and gave some directions to the driver, emphasizing her words with a pair of plump little hands. Then, with a "*bon nuit*," she disappeared, and the great doors closed again. Evidently we were being taken care of, we thought, as we settled back again in the carriage. We stopped before another door, already open, and disclosing a flight of wide, stone stairs, ascending almost from the sidewalk. Immediately upon pulling the bell — as though the wire had been attached to it — a long, loose-jointed, grotesque, yet horrible figure appeared at the head of the stairs, half-stooping to bring himself within the range of my vision, swinging his arms like a Dutch windmill, and grinning in a way which seemed to open his whole head.

"Is — is this Miss H.'s?" I ventured from the sidewalk.

He only beckoned still more wildly for me to ascend. I drew back. Good Heavens! What was the matter with him? And still, while I stared fascinated, yet horror-stricken, he continued, without intermission, these speechless contortions and evolutions. Although he uttered not a sound, he seemed to say with every cracking joint, "Come up, come up," while he scooped the air with his bony hands.

I remembered that it was midnight; that we were alone, and in wicked Paris; that we had been religiously brought up; that Mrs. K.'s husband was the superintendent of a large and flourishing Sunday school; that my father was a minister of the gospel. I planted my feet firmly upon the sidewalk. I folded my arms rigidly. I shook my head virtuously. Come up? Chains should not drag me. Then I turned to the carriage.

"Mrs. K., do come and see this man."

She came. Together we stared at him with rigid and severe countenances.

"Dreadful!" said I, remembering the Sunday school.

"Together we stared at him with rigid and severe countenances."
Page 240.

"Awful!" said she, recalling the pious ancestors. And again we shook our heads at his blandishments to the point of dislocation. The driver, who had been all this time tipped back against a tree, began to show symptoms of impatience. Something must be done.

"Suppose you ask for some one who can speak English," suggested Mrs. K.

"Sure enough." And I did. With one last, terrible grimace the ogre's heels disappeared up the second flight of stairs.

There came down in a moment a thoroughly respectable appearing porter, who informed us, in English, that we were expected, our telegram having been received; though, through the ambiguity of its address, it had been sent first to a house below. The people there had promised to forward us, however, in case we followed the telegram. This accounted for the movements of the little portress.

The *ogre* proved to be a most good-natured *concierge*, who had been instructed to keep the door open in anticipation of our arrival.

So our fears had been but feathers, after all, blown away by a breath; our troubles only a dream, to be laughed over in the awakening.

Here the story of our journeying may end. The remaining distance, through the kindness of friends, new and old, was accomplished without difficulty or annoyance. We reached our own homes in due time, and like the princess in the fairy tales, "lived happily forever afterwards."

A few practical words suggest themselves here which would pass unnoticed in a preface — where, perhaps, they belong. First, in regard to the question often asked, " Can women travel alone through Europe?" Recalling our own experience, — too brief to serve as a criterion, — I should still say, "*Yes.*" We met, frequently, parties of ladies who had made the whole grand tour alone. In Switzerland we found English women, constantly, without escort. The care of choosing routes, of looking after baggage and buying tickets, of managing the sometimes complicated affairs attendant upon sight-seeing, with the vexations and impositions met with and suffered on every hand, no woman would voluntarily accept without great compensation, I am sure. But if she prefers even these cares to seeing nothing of the world, they can be borne, and the annoyances, to a great extent overcome, through patience and growing experience.

Then, if you start alone, or without being consigned to friends upon the other side, — which no *young* woman would think of doing, — you are almost sure to join, at different times, other parties, whose way is your own; and far preferable this is to making up a large company before leaving home — the members of which usually disagree before reaching the continent, and often part in mutual disgust. " There is nothing like travelling to bring out a person's real nature," say some. But this is untrue. Travelling develops, rather than reveals, I think, and under conditions favorable only to the worse side of one's nature. You are bewildered by the multitude of strange sights and ways; the very foundation of usages is broken up; you are putting forth physical exertions that would seem superhuman at home, and are mentally racked until utterly exhausted,— for there is nothing so exhausting as continued sight-seeing,— and at this point people say they begin "to find each other out."

An occasional period of rest— not staying within doors to study up the guide-books, but entire cessation from seeing, hearing, or doing— and a scrap from the mantle of charity, will save many a threatened friendship at these times. We learned to know our strength — how weak it was; and to await in some delightful spot, chosen for the purpose, returning energy, courage, and *interest;* for even that would be banished at times by utter weariness and exhaustion.

In former times, Americans fitted themselves out for Europe as though bound to a desert island. Wider intelligence and experience have opened their eyes and reformed their judgment; still, a word upon this subject will not be unwelcome, I am sure, to girls especially, who contemplate a trip over the ocean.

In the first place, your steamer outfit is a distinct affair. You are allowed to take any baggage you wish for into your state-room; but, if wise, you will not fill the narrow space, nor encumber yourself with anything larger than a lady's *hat box*, which may offer a tolerable seat to the stewardess, or visitors of condolence, in case seasickness confines you to berth or sofa. Even preferable to this is a flat, English portmanteau, which can be slipped under the lower berth. If you sail for Liverpool, you can leave this at your hotel there in charge of the head waiter until you return, and thus avoid the expense and care of useless baggage.

Its contents your own good sense will in a measure suggest. Let me add— a double gown or woollen wrapper, in which you may sleep, flannels (even though you cross the ocean in summer), merino stockings, warm gloves or mittens, as pretty a hood as you please, only be sure that it covers the back of your head, since you will ignore all cunning craft of hair dressing, for a few days at least, and even after you are well enough to appear at the table, perhaps. Bear in mind that the Northern Atlantic is a cold place, and horribly open to the wind *at all seasons of the year;* that you will live on the deck when not in your berth or at your meals, and that the deck of an ocean steamer partakes of the nature of a whirlwind. Fur is by no means out of place, and skirts should be sufficiently heavy to defy the gales, which convert everything into a sail. Take as many wraps as you choose — and then you will wish you had one more. A large shawl, or, better, a carriage-robe, is indispensable, as you will very likely lie rolled up like a cocoon much of the time. A low sea-chair, or common camp-chair, is useful to older people; but almost any girl will prefer a seat upon the deck itself; there are comfortable crannies into which no chair can be wedged.

By all means avoid elaborate fastenings to garments. A multiplicity of unmanageable "hooks and eyes" is untold torment at sea; and let these garments be few, but warm. You will appreciate the wisdom of this suggestion, when you have accomplished the herculean task of making your first state-room toilet.

If you are really going abroad for a season of *travel*, take almost nothing. You can never know what you will need until the necessity arises. If you anticipate, you misjudge. Your American outfit will render you an oddity in England. But do not change there, or you will be still more singular in Paris. It is as well to start with but one dress besides the one you wear on the steamer — anything you chance to have; a black alpaca, or half-worn black silk, is very serviceable. When you reach Paris, circumstances and the season will govern your purchases; and this same dress will be almost a necessity for constant railway journeys, rainy-day sight-seeing, and mule-riding in Switzerland. A little care and brushing, fresh linen, and a pretty French tie, will make it presentable — if not more — at any hotel dinner table.

A warm shawl or wrap of some kind you will need for evenings, — even though you travel in summer, — for visiting the cathedrals, which are chill as a **tomb**; and for weeks together among the mountains you will never throw it aside. But if you can take but one, *don't* provide yourself with a *water-proof*. They are too undeniably ugly, and not sufficiently warm for constant wear. If it rains slightly, the umbrella, which you will buy from force of necessity and example in England, will protect you; if in torrents, you will ride. Indeed, you will always ride, time is so precious, cab-hire so cheap, **and** distances so great in most foreign cities.

Lastly, let me beg of you to provide yourself with an abundant supply of patience and good-nature. Without these, no outfit is complete. Try to laugh at annoyances. Smile, at least. And do not anticipate difficulties. Above all, enjoy yourself, and then everybody you meet will enjoy you. And so good by, and " God bless us every one."

www.ingramcontent.com/pod-product-compliance
Lightning Source LLC
Chambersburg PA
CBHW021404230426
43666CB00006B/629